D1493354

THE SEXY, VIOLENT, EXTRAORDINARY
LIFE OF VIKKI LAMOTTA

Knockout!

Books by Thomas Hauser

General Non-Fiction
Missing
The Trial of Patrolman Thomas Shea
For Our Children (with Frank Macchiarola)
The Family Legal Companion
Final Warning: The Legacy of Chernobyl (with Dr. Robert Gale)
Arnold Palmer: A Personal Journey
Confronting America's Moral Crisis (with Frank Macchiarola)
Healing: A Journal of Tolerance and Understanding
Miscellaneous
With This Ring (with Frank Macchiarola)
A God To Hope For
Knockout (with Vikki LaMotta)

About Boxing
The Black Lights: Inside the World of Professional Boxing
Muhammad Ali: His Life and Times
Muhammad Ali: Memories
Muhammad Ali: In Perspective
Muhammad Ali & Company
A Beautiful Sickness
A Year At The Fights
Brutal Artistry
The View From Ringside
Chaos, Corruption, Courage, and Glory
The Lost Legacy of Muhammad Ali
I Don't Believe It, But It's True

Fiction
Ashworth & Palmer
Agatha's Friends
The Beethoven Conspiracy
Hanneman's War
The Fantasy
Dear Hannah
The Hawthorne Group
Martin Bear & Friends
Mark Twain Remembers
Finding The Princess

THE SEXY, VIOLENT, EXTRAORDINARY
LIFE OF VIKKI LAMOTTA

Knockout!

BY VIKKI LAMOTTA & THOMAS HAUSER

www.sportclassicbooks.com

Published in the United States of America by Sport Media Publishing Inc.,
Wilmington, Delaware, and simultaneously in Canada.

For information about permission to reproduce selections from this
book, please write to:
    Permissions
    Sport Media Publishing, Inc.,
    55 Mill St., Building 5, Suite 240
    Toronto, Ontario, Canada, M5A 3C4
    www.sportclassicbooks.com

Cover design: Paul Hodgson

Interior design: Greg Oliver
This book is set in Bembo.

ISBN-10: 1-894963-51-2
ISBN-13: 978-1-894963-51-0

          Library of Congress Cataloging-in-Publication Data

    LaMotta,Vikki, 1930–2005.
    Knockout! : the sexy, violent, extraordinary life of Vikki Lamotta
    / by Vikki LaMotta and Thomas Hauser.
    p. cm.
    ISBN 1-894963-51-2 (hardcover)
    1. La Motta, Jake—Family. 2. LaMotta,Vikki, 1930–2005. 3. Boxers
(Sports)—United States—Biography. 4. Boxers' spouses—United
States—Biography. I. Hauser,Thomas. II. Title.
    GV1132.L3L36 2005
    796.83092'2--dc22
    [B]
    2005033891

Printed in Canada

In memory of Vikki LaMotta
1930 – 2005

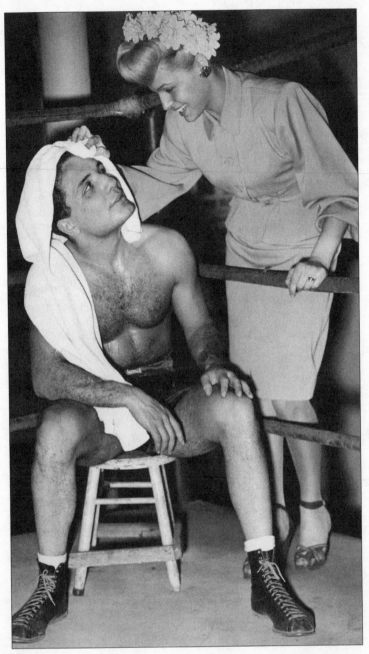

A fighter's wife.

Table of Contents

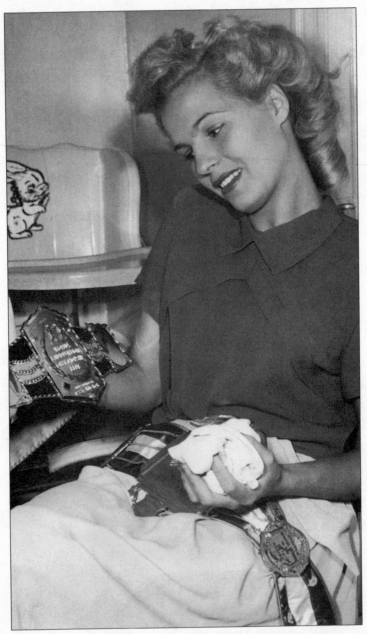

Polishing up championship gold.

A Word of Introduction

In 1984, I was introduced to Vikki LaMotta. I had just begun researching *The Black Lights*, which was my introductory work on professional boxing. Vikki was fifty-four and had achieved a measure of fame in a life that included experiences as diverse as having been married to Jake LaMotta and posing nude for *Playboy* at age fifty-one.

Like most people, I was impressed with Vikki's looks. Not only was she beautiful, she had a style that demanded attention. Heads turned when she walked by. For several years, we maintained a casual friendship. Then, in 1986, she asked if I'd be interested in collaborating with her on a book about her life.

The idea appealed to me. Vikki's story was like a highlight reel from a television mini-series. Born into poverty, married at age sixteen . . . Subjected to brutal beatings by her husband, world middleweight champion Jake LaMotta . . . She left Jake, worked as a chorus girl to support three young children, was pursued by Frank Sinatra, and became romantically involved with mob boss Sam Giancana . . . At one time or another, she'd crossed paths with the likes of Babe Ruth, Jimmy Durante, Johnny Carson, and Robert DeNiro. She had lived a lifetime of nightmares and dreams.

Vikki and I worked on the book in 1986 and 1987. We spent several months talking about her life, listening to audio tapes, and reviewing scrapbooks she had put together. During that time, she was painfully honest about some horrifying experiences that she had endured. When the manuscript was complete, we submitted it to publishers. We got an offer. Then Vikki got cold feet. She was uncomfortable with some of the revelations about her parents and other people she loved. "Maybe after I'm gone," she said.

At that point, I could have made a fuss. I'd put a lot of time and effort into the project. But I decided to let the matter drop. My satisfaction, such as it was, derived from the experience of writing and in a letter from Vikki that read as follows:

Dear Tom,

Life, final and complete. Once my past, dead, now alive forever. Packaged, small enough to carry under my arm. Not an edited life but honest facts and events.

After a final reading, a deep sigh with an amazing amount of relief and exhilaration. Not relief of a project completed but relief of a past saved, not lived in vain. Starting a new life combined with the past animated. Nurtured and cherished. I can hold it close, yet share it at the same time.

If anyone wants to know of my past, I'll just hand them my book. They can share it with me. The story has no message. It's only one person's experience in life. Good and bad. It is what it is. So be it.

Thank you, Tom. I love you.

Love,
Vikki

And that was that. I don't know if Vikki shared the manuscript with anyone else or not.

Time goes by. In February 2005, I read the sad news that Vikki LaMotta had died. Several weeks later, I received a telephone call from her son, Harrison Foster. Harrison told me that he had often asked his mother questions about her life. Sometimes, she'd given him answers. Other times, she had told him that, after her death, he could read about it in the manuscript we'd fashioned together,

But there was a problem. Harrison couldn't find the manuscript. Would I send him a copy?

I did, knowing that his mother's words would be a remarkable voyage of discovery for him.

After Harrison read the manuscript, he telephoned and said it would take a while for him to absorb everything he'd just learned. Then, in mid-2005, he asked if I would consider publishing the book as a way of honoring his mother.

These are Vikki's memories as she recounted them to me. Other than changing the names of a few childhood friends, I believe it is accurate and honest.

Vikki LaMotta was a good person. That's as simply and honestly as I can put it. She battled her demons and won. This is her story.

Thomas Hauser
September 2006

Vikki on the beach in her early teens.

Beginnings

Chapter One

People tell me I'm photogenic. It's meant as a compliment, but how I photograph has never mattered to me; except once, at age fifty-one, when I posed for *Playboy*.

"Try to be comfortable, Vikki . . . The bathing suit looks absolutely lovely . . . Lower the strap . . . Lift your right shoulder . . . Alright; now stand up . . . Head to the left . . . Higher . . . Arch your shoulders . . . Now lean forward."

After an hour, I didn't feel beautiful; not at all. I felt deformed. And the photo session had just begun.

Since then, I've spent a lot of time contemplating how I got to that point in my life. I have a certain type of looks; I attract attention. Being noticed is very much a part of who I am. Ever since adolescence, I've been an object of voyeurism; partly because of my face and body, and partly because of the way I've put myself on display. My appearance has affected me in a lot of ways, some of them bad. I've been sexually abused and subjected to beatings that brought me near death. I've worked as a chorus girl to support my children and been pursued by some of the most powerful men of our time. I'm trying now

15

to sort out the pieces that constitute my life; what happened, how it affected me, how I grew and changed. I've matured from a sixteen-year-old bride trying simply to survive into a woman determined never to be brutalized or exploited again. Now, finally, I have the tools to be happy. But I've made mistakes that I'm determined not to make again.

I was born in the Bronx on January 23, 1930. My father's parents were Romanian Jews, who immigrated to the United States in the late 1800s and had seven children; five boys and two girls. My father was the black sheep of the family. His brothers worked hard and saved their money. Julian owned a linoleum store. Herman was an ophthalmologist. Jack drove a cab, and Aaron crafted furniture. My father was a card-player. Not a professional gambler or big-stakes player; he gambled for fun. Most of the time, he broke even. But since he rarely held a job, his income was zero. Then he married my mother, a non-Jew, and was disowned completely. For years, I didn't know anyone on my father's side of the family. I didn't even know I was half-Jewish because he never practiced or spoke about religion. It wasn't until I was nine years old that a man named Marcus Thailer came to our door and asked for his son, Abe. That was my father's name, although everyone I knew called him "Feebie." The man was my grandfather, seeking reconciliation, and from then on I had an extended family. But my father still wouldn't work, and we were always in need.

My mother was born in 1909 and raised in Poughkeepsie, New York. Everyone called her Margie, short for Margaret. Her father was a construction engineer. His name is actually on a bridge in the Hudson Valley. Her mother died soon after my mother was born. Except for an aunt named Nanny, I don't think I saw any of my mother's relatives more than once when I was growing up; not even my grandfather. But I do know the family was half-English, half-Irish, and all Catholic.

Growing up, I thought of my mother as a beautiful woman. She had black hair, dramatic dark brown eyes, and a stunning figure. She wasn't tall; five-foot-three at most. But she was classically proportioned; smallwaisted with gorgeous legs and beautifully-shaped breasts. She always tried to make her breasts appear smaller than they were and never wore anything low-cut or showed off her curves. My father was proud of the way she looked. Whenever they had plans to go out together, he'd tell all the guys on the corner, "Margie is coming today." If she'd gotten fat, if her skin had broken out in a rash, he might not have been as proud. I sensed that. Her looks counted. He was proud to be with Margie because Margie was beautiful and "a perfect lady." She rarely gossiped or talked badly about anyone. She didn't have a lot of clothes, but what she wore was neat, clean, and fully starched. She had a pride and elegance about her to the point of being reserved and sometimes cold.

New York in the 1930s was very different from New York now. Jobs were scarce. The Great Depression was in bloom. We lived in a red brick building at 1078 Southern Boulevard near the corner of Westchester Avenue where the elevated subway turned. It was a tenement, five stories tall with four families on each floor. Our apartment had a kitchen, living room, and two bedrooms. My mother and father slept in an alcove off the living room. My brothers, Harvey and Don, who were a year older and younger than me, slept in one bedroom. I slept in the other with my younger sisters, Phyllis and Pat. There was one bed in each room. I shared a bed with my sisters until I got married.

The neighborhood was mostly Irish with some Jewish and Italian families thrown in. There were a few Hispanics and no blacks. People didn't bother to lock their doors. It wasn't a frightened society the way New York is now. The policemen all walked a beat. Everyone knew who they were. Each street had a bookmaker, who operated out of a coffee shop or luncheonette. Like the cops, they knew what was going on and they protected the neighborhood. If there was a robbery, which was rare, the victim's family could go to the bookmaker and, for some reason, the stolen items would reappear. They were the mob, of course; the bookmaking arm of the mob. But they were protection for the neighborhood as well. The cops were Irish; the bookmakers, Italian and Jewish. They got along.

People knew what was happening in their neighbors' lives. As a child, all I had to do was look out the window at other people's wash strung from clotheslines to tell who had company, who was home, who was away, and who had the cleanest laundry. Women were known by how often they did the wash. It was a status symbol, who did the best laundry.

An endless range of street characters marked our lives. The "Rag Man" rode by twice a week in a horse-drawn wagon, calling out, "We buy old clothes." If a family had clothes which couldn't be worn anymore, they'd bring them down. He'd pay pennies for the rags. The "Paper Man" did the same for bundles of paper wrapped together. The "Song Man" walked down the street, stopping in backyards to sing *Pennies From Heaven*, and people with money would throw coins out the window.

Modern appliances were rare. We didn't have a telephone. Once a day, the ice man came by. He rode a big wagon with gigantic chunks of ice piled high. My mother would tell him what size piece we needed for the kitchen. He'd split a slab in two with a chisel and carry whatever we needed upstairs in a canvas bag. During the winter, we saved money by putting our food in a box on the window ledge and using the outdoors as a refrigerator.

We were poor. That's the simplest way to describe our condition. My father simply refused to work. Occasionally, he'd take an odd job. At Christmas, he'd go down to the newsstand underneath the elevated subway and sell evergreens for a week or so. On Christmas Eve, if there were trees left over, he'd bring one home. Most of the time though, he played cards; poker, gin rummy, and pinochle. Where he got the money, I don't know. Gamblers always seem to have enough money to play; never enough for anything more. Each day, he was supposed to give my mother a dollar before he left to play cards. That was how we survived. Sometimes though, he wouldn't leave the dollar and there'd be literally no food at home. My mother would say to me, "There's no money for food; your father didn't leave the dollar." When that happened, I'd run after him. I couldn't have been more than seven or eight years old, but I knew where the men hung out and gambled. I'd find him, walk in, and my father would be sitting at a table with stacks of bills in front of him. I wouldn't say anything; I didn't interrupt. I'd just stand behind him until he was so embarrassed that he gave me the dollar. Then I'd go home a hero. "You got it!" my mother would cry out. "That's wonderful! You got the dollar!"

We survived, although some times were harder than others. One Christmas Eve, I stayed up waiting for Santa Claus. I really believed. I sat by the window, watching, looking for reindeer. Finally I fell asleep and, in the morning when I woke up, there was nothing. No tree; no presents; nothing. "Maybe Santa got hurt," my mother told me. "Or maybe he had too many people to visit last night." Then she started crying, and I realized the reason there weren't any presents was that my father didn't have a job.

Whenever my mother cried, I'd try to comfort her and she'd act as if it wasn't so: "Oh, it's not that; I'm not crying. There's something in my eye." After a while, I learned to go along with the pretense because I wanted to preserve her pride. I'd never say, "Mother, you're crying." Instead, I'd feel privileged to help her pretend. That's a heavy burden for a child to carry, and on this particular Christmas I didn't want to bear it at all.

That morning, for the first and last time in my life, I went begging. At least, that's how it seemed. In those days, the police gave presents to needy children on Christmas day. A little before noon, I went to the precinct house with my brothers, Harvey and Don. I'd never been embarrassed about being poor before, but this time I felt uncomfortable and shy. I guess some of my mother's pride had worn off on me. I didn't want the other children to know that I had to go to the police station to get a toy.

Inside the station house, about thirty children were waiting on line. They had a big Christmas tree and, beneath it, piles of toys. Some were wrapped; others were toys that people had donated because they'd been broken or outgrown. The police were jolly, in a happy frame of mind. Each child was given a toy at random when he or she reached the front of the line. Waiting, getting closer to the tree, I wanted a doll. I didn't ask; I just took what they gave me—a doll with a pink dress and reddish-brown hair, all curls. It was the first doll I'd ever owned. I was happy to have it. I also promised myself I'd never go back to the police station for a present again.

During those years, it was my mother who kept the family going. I think my father loved her. He'd never leave the house without kissing her goodbye. But he didn't really look after her. She was the one who had to face the problems each day, while he played cards as though the problems weren't there.

One of my most vivid memories of childhood is of my mother at the washtub, scrub-board in hand. It seemed as though she was always washing, and it wasn't until I got older that I learned she took in other people's laundry to make do. Summer, autumn, whatever the season, she seldom left the apartment. During the cold days of winter, the wash would be frozen into odd shapes when she brought it in from the laundry line. Another women who lived in our building worked in a garment factory and brought piecework home for my mother to work on in her spare time.

"Make do." In some ways, that was the watchword of my formative years. When there was nothing else to eat for dinner, my mother would make do by fashioning dumplings out of flour, salt, pepper, and water. When I needed paste for work in school, we used the same flour and water. In winter, as a special treat, she'd make ice cream from snow, evaporated milk, vanilla extract, and sugar. There was a government program called "home relief" which provided assistance to needy families but my mother refused to apply for it, saying she'd rather go hungry than accept "charity" from anyone.

Starting around age nine, I chipped in by doing odd jobs. My favorite was stuffing my hair under a cap, putting on Harvey's clothes, and going out on the street as a shoeshine boy. In some ways, it made me feel like the man of the family. Yet through it all, I rarely felt deprived. Whatever happened, the apartment we lived in was always spotless. The linoleum tile might be worn through to the boards below, but it was clean. My clothes were made out of leftover material, but the way my mother fitted and starched each dress, they were beautiful. My shoes had holes and cardboard inserted over the soles but they were polished. Whatever we did get, I was grateful for. And if there was something extra, extra food, extra money, it was thrilling.

Sometimes I'd ask myself, why isn't my father providing for us like other fathers? My friends, no matter how poor their families were, always had food to eat. That seemed like a luxury to me. I'd go to people's homes for dinner, and it was like a banquet, just having food on the table. I'd see other fathers going to work and the discrepancy was obvious. But still, I couldn't bring myself to question my father for not having a job. Instead, I'd tell myself, "This is our life; this is my father. That's the way things are."

My mother and father never fought that I know of. I never heard her yelling at him, "Why don't you get a job?" Instead, she suffered silently. The only outburst of emotion I remember came once when we got a radio on an installment plan. It was fantastic. We finally had a radio. We'd sit on the floor, turn out the lights, really prepare as a family to listen to *Inner Sanctum, Suspense,* and *Lux Radio Theater.* Then the store repossessed the radio because we couldn't make the payments. They took it away, and my mother was more upset than I'd ever seen her. She would have been a perfect rich lady, dressed in silk with tea and crumpets every afternoon. But instead, she had to accept the fact that the man she married wasn't a man who'd hold a job. What she got was who she married; Feebie, with his pluses and minuses.

Meanwhile, despite his shortcomings, just about everyone in the neighborhood seemed to like my father. He was "the mayor of the block"; gregarious, outgoing, always available to have a good time with the guys. Physically, he was five-foot-seven, with an athlete's build, broad shoulders, and strong hands. He had a wonderful smile and laughing eyes. He didn't care much about clothes, dressed in work pants and plaid flannel shirts, and never wore a tie. Most men wore hats in those days. My father scorned hats and only wore a coat when it was freezing cold. He loved cigars but rarely drank and was drunk only once in his life that I remember. We were at a picnic. He drank too much, got into a fight, came home sick, and threw up in the toilet. I was nine years old; I thought he was dying. I never saw him touch a drop again. Sometimes, I wonder if my father thought of himself as a failure. I doubt it. I honestly believe he loved his gambling and loved what he was doing. I never saw any remorse in him for that part of who he was.

Given what I've said so far, my childhood might have seemed bleak, but most of the time I was very happy. I loved being around people. I was always inquisitive. I never wanted to go to bed at night. Who could sleep? I was excited by life. The only way I'd go to sleep was if I passed out.

The windows of our apartment were level with the elevated subway tracks. I spent hours on our fire escape, watching trains roll by, imagining who the passengers were and where they were going. I loved to explore. I couldn't wait to go outside. There was a butcher shop across the street from where we lived. I'd watch how they cut the meat and ask, "Why do you do it that way? How come there's sawdust on the floor?" Next door, they made cigars; flattened the tobacco and rolled it onto leaves in the window. "Why do you do this? Why do you do that? Can I smell the tobacco?"

During the summer, I'd go up to the roof—tar beach, we called it—play in the sun, and jump from one building to the next. Winters, I was happy taking a sled downhill and veering left at the corner just before I hit the street with heavy traffic. Once, I started a fire in the apartment. I didn't realize what I was doing. I took some napkins, cut them into little pieces of paper, and lined them up on the floor. The idea was to light the first piece and have a nice chain of fire from one piece to the next like falling dominoes. The fire spread to the curtains before my father was able to put it out.

I loved being outdoors. Regardless of the season, I had to be outside. April through September were the best months because the days seemed longer and I didn't have to wear a coat. Most of my friends weren't allowed to leave the neighborhood. They were "too young" according to their parents, so I'd go alone. I'd visit swimming pools in black areas of the Bronx and stand in line with black and Hispanic children. Day after day, I was out on my own, staying out until dark. Once, I decided unilaterally to visit my father's parents. I knew they lived near Pelham Parkway, not far from the El, so I started walking, just following the elevated tracks above. It was a long walk; miles and miles. At one point, I came to a huge grassy field. There was a pretty white ball lying nearby, so I picked it up and a man ran over screaming, "You little thief, don't steal that ball." It was a golf range. I'd never seen one before. I didn't know what a golf ball was. By the time I got to my grandparents, it was almost dark.

That's the way I was. I'd explore and get excited about any number of things. "She's missing again," was a common refrain when my mother was talking about me. And then she'd send someone out onto the street to find out where I was.

Around the time I was eight years old, I discovered a vest-pocket park with a cast iron fence where the cab drivers lined up for fares. I'd go there, hang out, and listen to the cabbies talk. After a while, they got used to my being around. I wasn't a nuisance. I never repeated things I heard them say. I'd just be there, listening. And I loved it. I loved their conversations. These were men. They were out in the world where things were exciting. All of my mother's friends talked about nonsense: "Guess what Antoinette did today. Can you imagine? I'm buying the most beautiful white dress for communion. Two tablespoons of sugar and one cup of flour." . . . Enough! Please! Straight to the cab stand to find out what was happening with Joe Louis and the Brooklyn Dodgers, who bet how much on which number and who won. My mother's friends would come over wearing new dresses made out of beautiful material and not want me to touch. Okay, lady, if that's how you feel, Willie the cab driver will let me wear his hat for at least an hour.

There was a place called Harry's Bar & Grill, opposite the cab stand, where the cabbies would go for a beer each day around noon. It didn't hurt that Harry gave away free cheese and crackers with every draft. Women and children simply didn't go to Harry's. But after a while, I was invited with the cab drivers. The cheese and crackers were my best meal of the day and the conversation was wonderful. Baseball, football, basketball, boxing. This guy will win. No, that one will. You're wrong; so and so is better.

Finally, a few of the cabbies started taking me on calls. A passenger would get in the back seat. I'd sit in front, and we'd be off. Those were my first trips to good neighborhoods, and I was stunned by how other people lived. The children dressed differently. Lawns were manicured. Fences were painted and unbroken. The streets didn't have garbage on them. Every new neighborhood gave rise to a million questions. It was a thrill just to be riding in the cab.

Of all the drivers, the one I liked most was Willie Goldberg. He was a short heavy man in his late thirties, kindhearted, very lonely. Whatever the weather, he wore a peak cap, white shirt and tie, with a sweater over the tie. Willie sort of adopted me to make up for the children he didn't have. And I sensed, even as an eight-year-old, that I was probably his best friend. I adored him.

Willie was always bringing me on calls. Every Wednesday during the summer, his day off, he'd take me for ice cream. After we'd known each other about a year, he realized I was crazy about a jacket he had: A baseball jacket made of royal blue satin, the kind major league players used to wear. Willie went out and bought me one with my name embroidered in red thread. Then he started taking me to movies at the Paradise Theatre on the Grand Concourse; and I was in heaven, looking at the ceiling which was covered with bright twinkling stars.

There was one thing Willie wanted in life besides a family—his own cab. He wanted a medallion. That's what he was working for. He'd explain to me what a medallion was, what it cost, and how, if he had one, he'd own his own cab and wouldn't have to share fares with anyone. Finally, he got it. Then, just after he turned forty, he had a heart attack and died.

Willie Goldberg helped fill a void in my life, but he couldn't do it alone. I can recall as a child wishing my mother and father would do things with me the way other parents did with their children. My mother never took me to the park when I was young. My father and I never went to movies together. The things that I did alone when I was eight or nine were things most children that age did with their parents.

I loved my brothers and sisters but didn't really spend much time with them. Sometimes I felt like the little match girl; especially during the winter months, when it was cold and dark and I was out on the streets alone. The deprivation I felt wasn't financial or material. Those liabilities, I accepted completely. The deprivation was not having anyone to share things with in the way I wanted to share. When a child is through playing on the streets, when he or she is finished for the day, if the child can't share the day with family, then that child is alone. And the truth is, I wasn't able to share large portions of my life with my family at that age; not with my parents; not with my brothers or sisters.

Sometimes I cried, but only when I was alone. And when I did, I'd try hard to stop. Occasionally, I'd actually get matches and emulate what the little match girl did to stay warm. I'd be outside, go into a doorway, light a match, and hold it to my face to feel the heat and see the glow. But in the end, I always had to go home.

My mother was very withholding and stand-offish; never openly affectionate or warm. She was always proper and polite, doing "the right thing" such as it was. But I can't remember her ever saying she loved me. Neither of my parents showed much physical affection. I was rarely hugged. There were small things that one or the other would do that gave me a sense of belonging. Simple acts which made me feel they cared or a look of love in their eyes. But for the most part, the emotional environment was silent and closed. That was made dramatically clear by an event that occurred when I was ten years old.

The one person on my mother's side of the family who I was close to was her Aunt Nanny. Nanny was wonderful; fiercely independent but gentle and kind. She'd been married once and her husband died young before they could have children. She was about as eccentric as a woman could be and looked like a kindly witch with a gaunt face and huge beaked nose. Her long gray hair was always twisted on top of her head and held in place by an oversized pin. She wore old house dresses, and kept her money in a stocking tied to her bra. Every time Nanny needed money, she'd untie the stocking and reach in to dig out the cash. She lived in Poughkeepsie, a small town in upstate New York, in the back room of a dilapidated second-hand clothes store she operated and owned. I didn't visit as often as I'd like, but every day we spent together was spectacular. I'd climb trees and Nanny would stand beneath me. If it rained, I'd go outdoors to run around in the puddles, and Nanny would be there.

One day, in the summer of 1940, I was in Poughkeepsie and Nanny said, "I'm going to take you somewhere. I want you to meet someone." We got on a train and rode to Troy, New York. Then, from the train station, we went to a hill overlooking a school building that Nanny told me was an orphanage called The LaSalle Institute For Boys. Several teenagers dressed in shorts, sneakers, and tank tops were playing basketball in the schoolyard. Nanny pointed to one—sixteen years old, tall, very good-looking with blue eyes and jet black hair—and told me, "That's your brother, Joe."

My brother, Joe?

I didn't understand. I knew I had brothers named Harvey and Don; and two sisters, Phyllis and Pat. But Joe? Nanny and I went down the hill, and she told the school officials that we were there. They sent Joe over to see us. I was ten years old; more excited than I'd been in my life. Joe was wonderful; like a Greek god.

The next day, I went back to New York. And like any ten-year-old, I couldn't contain myself. "I met my brother Joe; he's incredible. I'm so happy." And my mother acted like I wasn't saying anything; like I wasn't there. So of course, I went out and told everyone in the neighborhood, "I have an older brother. He's fantastic; he's handsome; he's sixteen years old."

And my mother still wouldn't acknowledge Joe's existence.

Years later, I pieced the story together a little more. When my mother was fifteen, she bore a child out of wedlock. I don't know who the father was, except it was someone she knew well; someone close to the family, who spent a lot of time in the home; maybe a relative. The child was born in 1924 at St. Francis Hospital in Poughkeepsie, a facility staffed by nuns from the order of St. Joseph. My mother never tried to raise Joe. Instead, she pretended the pregnancy hadn't happened, that he wasn't there. Immediately after he was born, she left him with Nanny, who acted as Joe's "mother" and visited him wherever he was.

Several months after Joe was born, my mother came to New York to live with relatives. It was then that she met my father. He was kind to her, and two years older than she was. At the time, he was working as a lifeguard. She told him about the child before they were married, and they agreed that Joe would stay where he was. If it weren't for Nanny, I never would have known about him. What happened afterward, though, was that Nanny's "indiscretion" opened a new world for us all. From then on, every time I saw her, I'd ask, "How's Joe? Tell me about Joe." Then, in January 1943, Joe enlisted in the Coast Guard and came to New York on leave. My mother was ambivalent but my father told him, "You're always welcome. Come, bring your friends. I want you in our home."

That was Feebie, the good warm side of him; the man who loved people and said to Joe, "Anytime you're in New York, our home is your home." And that was my mother: very closed, a cold-starer, strong in her silence; unwilling to face up to problems; dedicated to the rule that impressions govern. I suppose I understand why she acted the way she did toward Joe. In the 1920s, it was a disgrace for a woman to have a child out of wedlock. The experience must have been horrifying for her, and I'm sure it went a long way toward molding who she was: a woman whose pride and self-image precluded her from seeking aid or solace. But there was an element of hypocrisy about her as well. When I was a child, she used to tell me, "Anytime you have a problem, you can come to me and discuss it." But the truth is, she didn't face up to problems; not mine, not her's, not anyone's.

Years later, I'd listen to my mother talk about certain types of unacceptable conduct. "Oh, I'd never do that," I'd hear her say. "I would never act in that fashion." And I'd tell myself, "Wait a minute. Look at Joe. Whatever airs you have, look at the way you treated him. All Joe wants before he dies is to know who his father was, and you won't tell him. Look at Joe. He could have been such a joy in your life if only you'd been willing to let him in."

Chapter Two

Like all children, I was shaped by family. And like all children, I was influenced by school. The elementary school I attended was predominantly white with a handful of black and Hispanic children mixed in. I did fairly well, with one problem: I couldn't see the blackboard. Time and again, teachers would write problems on the board and ask, "What's the answer?" I wouldn't know. I needed glasses but didn't realize my eyesight was bad. Other children could give the answers. "How do they solve the problems?" I wondered. "I must be stupid because they understand what's going on and I don't." My grades were respectable because I was adept at maneuvering and had native intelligence. By keeping quiet about what I didn't understand, I was able to avoid embarrassment. Then came seventh grade, and my world was turned upside down.

Under local zoning requirements, children from my neighborhood were supposed to attend Junior High School 60 in a district which encompassed Longwood Avenue (mostly Hispanic) and Prospect Avenue (mostly black). I say "supposed to" because the great majority of white parents found a way to enroll their children in other schools. Either they had enough money for private school education, which was rare since it was a poor neighborhood, or else they lied about where the family lived. My mother sent me to the junior high school for which we were zoned. That was the "proper" way.

Virtually all the black and Hispanic kids at JHS 60 had gangs. The white girls (it was an all-girls school) didn't. After I'd been there about a week, one of the black kids said something to me in the schoolyard, and I answered back. I don't remember what it was. Probably, we were mouthing off about nothing, but white girls made up less than twenty percent of the student body and we were supposed to know our place. The next day, a group of black girls was waiting for me after school. Lucille Simpson was the leader. She was in ninth grade, two years older than I was. She was built like a boy, big and strong with broad shoulders and close-cropped hair; a head taller than I was. Lucille didn't say anything. She just walked up to me with her friends around her and punched me in the eye.

I went wild. It was the first time in my life that anyone had hit me to hurt me, and I went crazy. I wasn't rational. I went at her to kill. She was bigger than I was and strong enough to hold me, but I kept kicking and screaming and she had her hands full trying to control me. Finally, some teachers came into the schoolyard and pulled us apart. The next day, I was afraid to go back to school. I had an ugly black eye. I was convinced that Lucille and her gang would be waiting for me. I went anyway; I had no choice. But I had to come up with something in order to survive, and then the solution became clear. I'd show the black and Hispanic girls that I was as tough as they were. I'd be just as bad, if not worse. I'd talk back to teachers; walk out of classes, be a leader. All to protect myself.

I was twelve years old.

I became them. My schoolwork suffered but I was accepted. Mostly, I hung out with a group of Puerto Rican girls. I'd go to their homes, meet their relatives, and listen to Latin music. I even developed a Spanish accent. Then the black girls befriended me too. Now I was bigtime; a real leader. Once, a group of us went to a department store to shoplift. The other girls were stealing little things; a comb, a mirror. I walked out with a green tweed double-breasted wool coat. I couldn't take it home. I'd never be able to explain to my parents where it came from, so I gave it to one of the other girls. That made me an even bigger hero.

The white kids in the school weren't part of my life anymore. But no one fought with me again because, if they had, every black and Hispanic gang member in the school would have jumped them. My whole identity changed; even my name. My real name was Beverly Rosalyn Thailer. One day, my Puerto Rican friends and I got together and said, "Let's change our names. You be this, and you be that." Everyone was getting a new name. "You be Carmen. For you, Rosa is right." When my turn came, somebody said, "You should be Vikki."

I was Vikki from then on. The other girls dropped their new names in about a month, but Vikki stayed with me. After a while, even my parents started calling me Vikki Thailer. But there were other aspects of my new identity that they wouldn't accept. For the first time, my mother was being called to school to meet with the principal and teachers about my conduct. I was saying the wrong things and acting the wrong way at home. Both of my parents despised the element I'd become involved with. The only solution, as my mother saw it, was moving to a new neighborhood to get me into a better school. And to afford that, my father had to get a job.

Finally, when I was thirteen, he relented and went to work as a butcher for Joe Weinberg at Joe's Meat Market. Soon after, we moved to 165th Street and Longfellow Avenue in the Bronx. But by then, I wasn't about to conform. I'd learned to be flamboyant; how to make other girls come to me and want to be my friend. As soon I started eighth grade at Junior High School 93, I became a leader. Each morning, a group of girls would wait outside the school for my instructions: "Okay; we're going to class today," or "No school; we're taking the subway downtown. We're going to this dance tonight and the beach tomorrow afternoon."

I graduated from eighth grade in January 1944, a few days before I turned fourteen. What I remember most about the ceremony is that each graduate had to go up on the stage to receive a diploma, and I'd told my mother I wanted to graduate in high heels. She bought me a pair; closed shoes, black leather, the first heels I'd ever owned. My feet were killing me and I wobbled all over the place, but somehow I managed to get on and off stage without falling down.

Meanwhile, at home, the joy that seemed just around the corner when my father got a job wasn't there. He was working, but not at all satisfied. My mother had some income but little more. A lack of communication pervaded my life. Nothing of importance was ever discussed with my parents. The children weren't even allowed to speak during dinner other than, "Please pass the potatoes" or "May I be excused?" And too much of my existence was shrouded in confusion, especially in light of my growth toward sexual maturation. As a child, I'd never thought about my looks. Occasionally, I'd overhear one of my mother's friends saying, "Your daughter will be beautiful," and my mother would answer, "I don't think so." Or someone would say, "Vikki has perfect features," and my mother would respond, "Not really."

I didn't know what I looked like, good or bad. Around the time I turned fourteen, the men who'd always treated me as a mascot started to act differently. There were comments and funny glances, but by then I was used to attention. Don't forget, I'd been the ringleader in school. Now that I was coming of age and men paid attention to me, I thought it was my personality. That's the truth. My upbringing hadn't focussed on appearance. I don't remember looking in a mirror to study my face or body until after I got married. My sisters and I didn't even undress in front of one another at night. There'd been no discussion about sex beyond a few lectures from my mother about menstruation. Years later, people told me that, from the time I was fourteen till the time I was thirty, I looked twenty. I don't know if that's true or not; but at fourteen, I didn't know that men and women thought I was beautiful. My mother said I wasn't, and that was that.

Every now and then, a discomforting incident would occur. Once, I was with a friend, Ellen Waters, who was several years older than I was. We were at her apartment with her boyfriend, and he made some comment about her breasts. Ellen said, "You should see Vikki's breasts. Her body is really beautiful." I was embarrassed. The guy was saying, "Yeah. Why don't you show me?" And Ellen was pushing, "Show him. I just want him to see how beautiful you are."

I didn't do it, but I was confused. Meanwhile, for the first time, my father was starting to act strangely toward me. For most of my life, he'd shown very little interest in what I did. Now, all of a sudden, he was telling me what to do; not advice, not discussions, but orders: "Do this; don't do that. Be home by nine o'clock, or else." I started to rebel. I wouldn't conform to what he wanted me to do. My brothers and sisters did. Even though they might not believe he was right, they went along and were rarely punished. To me, that meant they were being dishonest, acting in a way they didn't feel. I refused to do that. I'd say what I felt; do what I thought was right and wanted to do. I didn't really date. There were a few boys I thought were cute, but no one I had a crush on or was lovesick over. Almost always, I'd go with a group when I went out. We'd go to a dance or the beach. If there was a boy I liked a lot, maybe we'd sit on a bench and kiss but nothing more.

Then the beatings started at home.

The first one came after I went to a dance at St. Helena's Church. I had come home late several nights that month, the last time ten minutes late, and my father told me I couldn't go out for two weeks. That seemed ridiculous, grounded for two weeks because I was ten minutes late. So I defied him. I went to the dance anyway. And when I got home, my father was waiting, beside himself with rage. He had never hit me before; maybe a spanking when I was little, but that was all.

This time, he walked toward me without a word, raised his fists, and hit me. And then he kept hitting me. That's what a beating is. It's not a flash explosion or one punch in anger. It's sustained punishment. He punched me; I moved away. He'd catch up and punch me again. I couldn't believe it was happening. This was my father!

The beatings lasted for about a year. Always, the pattern was the same. I'd go to a dance, come home late, and be beaten. I didn't think I was doing anything wrong. All that happened was, I'd get home late. The subway wouldn't be on time or my girlfriends would want to stay at the dance a few minutes extra. We didn't have a telephone, so I couldn't call home to say I'd be late. And after a while, I'd tell myself, "He's going to beat me anyway, so why not stay out as late as I want." Sometimes I'd be so afraid to go home that, when I reached our building, I'd go up to the roof and sit there for hours rather than face my father.

All totalled, he beat me at least a dozen times. For a while, he used fists. Then he became embarrassed that I was going to school with bruises on my face so he took a hose—a heavy orange hose with ridges on it from an old wringer washing machine—and started beating me with that. There were still marks, big ugly welts, but they were on my back so people couldn't see them. Other times, he'd kick me with the boots he wore at Joe's Meat Market. I took it defiantly. I never hit back, never scratched or clawed. I'd just take it to show him I couldn't be broken. And I took it silently. I refused to cry out until one time he was so enraged by my silence that he told me, "I'm going to make you cry." He hit me hard, again and again, until I saw black from the pain, screamed, and broke down sobbing. Finally, Feebie had made me cry. And then, to get even, I went out again.

Those beatings were the first time in my life that I was aware of suffering. I felt degraded, embarrassed, and betrayed by my father. My brothers and sisters knew what was going on. They could hear from the next room but they never objected. My mother acted as though it wasn't happening and never did anything to protect or comfort me. And the craziest thing was, even as my father was beating me, I felt sorry for him. I'd tell myself, "He's causing more pain for himself than he is for me." On occasion, I'd even go to the meat market to have lunch with him. And then, sometimes as soon as the next night, the beatings would resume: "He's hurting me! What can I do? As long as he beats me and I don't strike back, I'm the one with the true moral power."

Was I angry? You bet I was! And I fought back by going out again and again until, finally, I got my victory. I broke him.

It happened just after I turned fifteen. My father was angry at me for cutting classes, and he started yelling, "Vikki, you know something? You get a balloon; you huff and you puff and you blow the balloon up. And you huff and puff and then, bang, the balloon explodes. That's what you're doing to me. You're making me explode."

I started to laugh. And my father got furious, angrier than I'd ever seen him. I couldn't stop laughing; I was literally hysterical. Then he looked at me and said, "Get a scissors; I'm cutting off your hair."

I'm sure he wanted me to plead and beg, to say, "Don't do it. I'll go to class. I'll come home on time. I'll do anything." But instead, I told myself, "I can't stand this anymore. Let him do it; get it over with."

I went into the bedroom and got the scissors.

My father ordered me to sit on the floor between his legs. Then he cut off all my hair. At first, I thought he was going to cut it shorter by two or three inches. Then I realized it wasn't that at all. The first cut went right to my scalp. Then another, and another. His hands were trembling and I was afraid he'd draw blood. I sat there with my eyes open, defiant. Minutes before, I'd had thick beautiful below-the-shoulders hair. And now I was virtually bald. It was mutilation.

When he was finished, I went into the bedroom. My mother didn't come in, even though she knew what had happened. And then, suddenly, everything hit me. I ran to the mirror, stared at myself, and realized, "Oh my God! I have no hair."

Somehow, I got by. In a few days, I bought a bottle of peroxide and bleached the stubble blonde. Until then, I'd been a brunette. Then I went to the five-and-ten-cent store for some plastic flowers that I pinned to my hair. A week later, I bought a white turban like Lana Turner wore. People knew what had happened but it wasn't discussed; not in front of me anyway. I'm sure, behind my back, all the kids were saying, "Did you see what Vikki's father did to her?" But like the beatings, cutting off my hair was something I was too embarrassed to talk about.

It was also too embarrassing for my father to deal with. Everyone in the neighborhood knew what he had done. Everyone could see how he had mutilated his daughter. He was ashamed; and not being able to break me broke him.

After my father cut my hair off, he never touched me again.

Chapter Three

Looking back, even from a vantage point of more than forty years, it's hard to put my childhood and adolescence in perspective. I think my parents loved me. That might sound strange but I believe it's true. In fact, I was probably closer to my father than any of the other children were. Yes, he beat me, and he never hit anyone else that I know of. Yes, he could be cruel, and I don't know what demons were at work inside him. But through it all, I felt he cared.

During those years, my greatest resentment was aimed at my mother. How could she ignore what was going on? How could she sit there and not protect me? Her stated reason was that one parent shouldn't interfere with the other when a child is being disciplined, but that's nonsense. Then, years later, after my father had died, my mother told me she'd been afraid to intervene because of what she called my father's "mental problem." She referred to a series of scars on his left forearm; scars I'd seen as a child, scars my father had always refused to talk about. And she confessed that, around the time I'd been born, she'd wanted to leave my father but he'd threatened to kill himself if she did. He'd taken a knife and slashed himself four times. From that point on, she was afraid he'd make good on his threat of suicide.

I don't know if that's true or not. Growing up, I was never aware that my mother might leave my father. But I do know that the fear she wasn't a good mother haunted her in later years. I still have a letter she wrote me in 1962, shortly after I'd turned thirty-two years old. It's six pages long, handwritten. And in the middle, almost out of nowhere, she wrote, "The only guilt I feel is why wasn't I a good mother to all of you. If I had been, you children wouldn't have had so many problems. Perhaps I was too self-centered. I don't know the answers. I only know I truly loved you and did the best I knew how. If it was not right, what can I do now? It's too late for tears. I hope God forgives me."

So I guess what I'm saying is, my mother did the best she was capable of. She had a hard life, before and during her marriage. Her own mother died young. She herself lived through the trauma of having an illegitimate child. She raised five children with very little money or other support.

As for my father, he was who he was. Some people might look at him and see a compulsive gambler, a man who horribly abused his daughter, someone who refused to face up to his responsibilities and obligations. I never discussed any of that with him; not until the day he died. I wanted to believe in him; I still do. And yet, after the beatings stopped, my father continued to fail me. Because once he realized what he'd done, instead of coming to grips with the problem, he grew extreme in the opposite direction. He never tried to discipline or guide me at all. It was a time when I needed guidance, someone to talk with about life; and no one was there.

I was fourteen, and starting to have real problems with men. Inside the neighborhood, things were all right. The girls I hung out with were "good girls." The guys respected us. Every now and then, one of them would get fresh, but we were always able to draw the line. Outside the neighborhood, it was a different story. If a girl wasn't from a particular section of town, then the men there didn't know her. They only knew what she looked like and had no reason to respect her. After a while, I was afraid to leave my neighborhood. Men were constantly stopping me on the street and offering to drive me places in their cars. Not just boys my own age, but adults. They'd promise to buy me presents if I went out with them; and when I wouldn't, they'd plead, cajole, and sometimes threaten. More than once, I went to dances. I'd be talking with somebody from one gang; somebody from another gang would ask me to dance; and soon they'd be fighting. One night, I went to a dance at the Holy Name Church in lower Manhattan, and there was a knife fight. Someone was stabbed. Over nothing. I had to climb out a window to escape.

Then I fell victim to a far more terrifying moment. I'd never had a boyfriend. And more important, I was a virgin. The latter condition was of particular consequence. If a girl lost her virginity, and hence her reputation, she was in trouble. And, don't forget, these were days when there was little effective birth control for women. The pill and IUD were in the future. Abortion was illegal.

From time to time, Donna Coletta and I went swimming at Coney Island. She was my best friend, the same age as I was, attractive with hazel eyes and long sand-colored hair. One day at the beach, we got a lot of attention from two guys. We were fourteen. They were older, twenty-two or twenty-three. One was named Sal. He was about five-foot-nine, nice-looking, stocky and very strong. The other was named Joe. They were Italian, from the lower east side. Donna and I had seen them at Coney Island and talked with them before. This time, we spent all day with them and, when it was time to leave, Sal said, "You don't have to take the subway. We'll drive you home."

That was exciting, avoiding a long train ride and being driven home. We felt comfortable with them; so Donna and I got in the car, a black four-door sedan. On the way home, Sal said they had to pick something up in Greenwich Village. We stopped at a restaurant with a small bar and they suggested we have a drink. I said I didn't drink and Sal told me, "Well, have one soda." Then he ordered pink ladies for Donna and me, while he and Joe went off to discuss business with some people at the bar. I didn't know it, but I was having my first drink. The pink lady tasted like soda; I had two of them.

Now it was starting to get dark. The four of us got back in the car and Sal said, "Why don't you come to dinner with us? We'll stop at a place that's very nice. A rooftop restaurant; it's on the way home." Donna and I said okay. We drove twenty blocks to an old hotel, stopped the car, and went inside. I had no idea what a rooftop restaurant was supposed to look like. I didn't realize it should have a sign or some other identifying feature downstairs. We took the elevator to the top floor, got off, and Sal reached into his pocket for a key. Then he opened a door and pushed us into a suite of rooms. I was getting scared; but before I could do anything, Sal reached for Donna's arm, told her, "I want to talk with you," and led her through a door to another room inside. That left me alone with Joe, who told me, "Don't worry; nothing's going to happen. We're leaving soon." He actually seemed nice; I believed him. Then Sal came back with Donna. I don't think he'd touched her. I think he'd been telling her he wanted me.

Sal took my arm and started pulling me toward the

bedroom. Joe was trying to stop him: "Look, it's not nice. Leave her alone." By now, I was terrified: "You can't hurt me! I'm only fourteen!" Sal just pulled harder, dragged me into the room, kicked the door shut, and threw me on the bed. All I could do was cry, "I'm a virgin! Leave me alone!" Then he slugged me, right on the jaw, and knocked me unconscious. And while I was unconscious, he penetrated. By the time I came to, he was getting off me. My shirt and bra hadn't been touched. My slacks and panties were down to my knees. I was dazed and bleeding from my mouth and vagina. Sal got up from the bed and walked out of the room without a word.

There was a dresser in the bedroom with a mirror above. I looked to see what had happened. My face was swollen and streaked with blood. I went into the bathroom, took a towel, and started washing myself with cold water. I felt desperate, embarrassed, humiliated, and ashamed. All my life, I'd wanted to be a virgin for the man I married, and now I was unclean. Finally, I went back to the living room. Donna, Joe, and Sal were waiting. Joe looked sad but didn't say anything. "Come on," Sal ordered. "We're going."

We went downstairs on the elevator. Sal's car was parked at the curb. "I'll get you girls a cab," he said. And all the while, I was asking myself, "What should I do?" Then I saw the license plate on the car—4K452. I remember it to this day. Sal saw me looking, threw his jacket over the plate, and hailed a cab. He gave the driver money and told him to take us to the Bronx. As soon as the cab started moving, I told the driver, "I want to go to a police station." Then Donna started to cry. "You can't do that, Vikki. My mother will be furious. I don't want her to know."

Donna hadn't been raped. Her mother wasn't uppermost

in my thoughts. Then, on the way to the police station, I started to worry. Rape was a horrible thing. People looked down on a girl who'd been raped. It was her fault. If I went to the police, the first thing they'd do was tell my parents. Soon, everyone in the neighborhood would know. I could handle the embarrassment, but what about my mother? Why bring more suffering to her?

Why? Because I wanted Sal punished. I wanted him hurt for leaving me defiled and scared. Very scared, which, I realized, was why I couldn't go to the police after all. Sal was a hood; that was the way he'd acted. He knew where I lived. If he were arrested, there'd be repercussions from the mob. His people would come and hurt my family. And if my father knew I'd been raped, he'd go after Sal. My father was tough but he wasn't a thug. Sal could kill him.

"I've changed my mind," I told the cab driver. "Take us home."

In retrospect, I should have gone to the police. Going home left me with an even greater feeling of shame. I never confided in my parents about what had happened. The next day, my face was still swollen, and I told my mother I'd fallen off a ride at Coney Island. Then my cheek became infected and had to be lanced. I never saw Donna again. She'd been my best friend. I'd liked her a lot. But after the rape, I was too embarrassed to confront her. I stopped going to the places we'd hung out together. At school, I avoided her. Gradually, I withdrew from our mutual friends. And of course, I was more afraid than ever of men. I wouldn't date anyone alone. If I went out, it was only with a group of people.

One night, a group of guys took me to the 181 Club in lower Manhattan. There was a stage show with lots of beautiful women. When it was over, the owner of the club came to our table and asked if I'd like to work for him. Five nights a week, twenty dollars a night. I'd had jobs before. In eighth and ninth grade, I'd worked after school in a factory that manufactured designer combs. Summers, I'd been on an assembly line making Oreo cookies for the National Biscuit Company. The most I'd ever been paid was seventy-five cents an hour. Twenty dollars a night, a hundred dollars a week, seemed like a fortune.

I took the job. I was fifteen years old. Each night, the orchestra would play *A Pretty Girl Is Like A Melody* and I'd walk out on stage. I'd dance; that was all. Basically, I'd been hired to put myself on display, but they gave me such a beautiful evening gown to wear that I didn't mind. I'd never had a new dress in my life, and here I was, wearing a long black satin gown with a black velvet hood that was absolutely stunning. The show didn't even run late. I was home by midnight.

Then I started to feel uncomfortable. The main act was a man who dressed like a woman. He looked gorgeous but he was a guy. I discovered that all the waiters, who I thought were men, were actually women. I knew a little about lesbians and homosexuals, but how could a woman look so much like a man? They walked like men; they talked like men. I couldn't believe they were women.

The audience was made up of men and women. They came because it was a good show. I assumed the other chorus girls were straight, until one of them told me she was dating a waiter. The waiters were what really freaked me out. Flat-chested women with men's hair, dressed in black tuxedos with white shirts, black bow ties, and men's shoes. Then, after a few weeks, they changed the show to give me a bigger role. I was supposed to dance on stage with a really dykish woman who was dressed like a man. I couldn't handle it. Instead of just being confused and embarrassed, I began to get frightened, so I quit the job.

Those were hard years for me. Adolescence is a difficult time in life. It's a period when children need guidance; someone to say, "You shouldn't work in that nightclub"; someone to talk with about life and problems. Yet here I was, fifteen years old. I'd been beaten by my father and found no one to protect me. I'd been raped and hadn't told a soul what had happened. There was no one to turn to. I was unhappy and alone, learning everything the hard way, just trying to survive.

And then I met Jake.

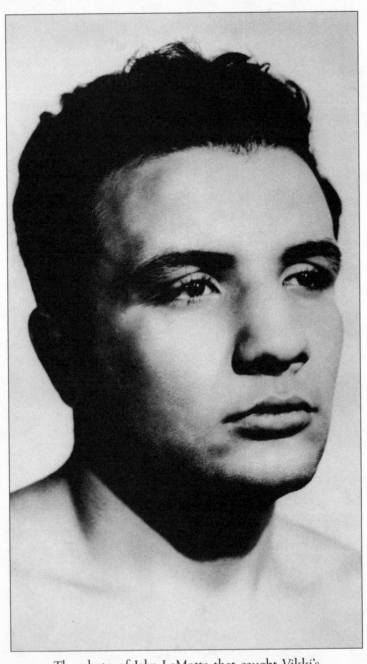

The photo of Jake LaMotta that caught Vikki's
eye before she ever met him.

Jake

Chapter Four

When I met Vikki, it was love at first sight. She was so pretty, just a baby. And I said to myself, that's mine, she belongs to me."

That was Jake, talking about the day we met. Possessive, wasn't he? What he didn't know was, I'd had a crush on him before he ever saw me.

It began when I was fifteen, going with my friends to Orchard Beach. Section nine was where we'd meet. The beach was divided with blacks in one area, Hispanics in another, and so forth. That year, I hung out with the Italians. One afternoon, a boy who'd been to the fights brought a souvenir program to the beach. I knew a fair amount about boxing from my days with the cabbies and my father had taken me to several bouts. I started leafing through the program, looking at the pictures of each fighter, and soon all the girls were looking at the photos with me to see who was cute.

Then I saw Jake's picture. His face seemed molded; his eyes, gentle and soft.

Jake LaMotta—"God, what a doll! Look at this picture!"

One of the boys volunteered the information that Jake was half-Jewish. That wasn't true. Jake was short for Giacobe, not Jacob. But at the time, his handlers were spreading the rumor that Jake's mother was Jewish to get Jewish support. And of course, I was half-Jewish too.

That was how I learned about Jake. The summer passed, and I went back to tenth grade at James Monroe High School in the Bronx. I studied enough to get by and, after classes, hung out at a luncheonette called The Sugar Bowl on Morris Park Avenue. Two or three afternoons a week, my friends and I would go there, drink malteds, play the juke box, and dance. There was an illegal poker game in back, but the men who played were busy gambling and left us alone. Then, one afternoon when they were coming out of the back room, I heard them talking about a fight; so-and-so against Jake LaMotta, who lived in the neighborhood. I couldn't believe it: "Jake LaMotta lives in this neighborhood?" And one of the men told me, "Sure, two blocks from here."

"Is he married?"

"Yes."

Right away, my fantasy vanished. Knights in shining armor weren't supposed to be married. Nice girls didn't date men who were already attached.

Then in the spring of 1946, my father bought a family pass for Castle Hill swimming pool in the Bronx. I was still wearing a turban because my hair hadn't grown out, but I had a sexy white bathing suit and had started to pose a bit. Each day, I'd go to the pool with my brothers and sisters and sit on the same concrete steps. There was another group that generally sat next to us, and pretty soon we were friendly with each other. One afternoon, a guy named Joey from the other group told me, "You know something? If my brother saw you, he'd fall in love. He'd really flip."

I didn't pay much attention. Joey was on the arrogant side and I didn't care much for him. But the next day, while I was sitting on the steps, he came by and said, "Come on; I want you to meet my brother." I followed him to a mesh wire fence that separated the pool area from the street. There, on the other side, was Jake—the same man whose picture had been in the boxing program. Soft eyes; shy and laid back. There was nothing pretentious or brazen about him. He was wearing street clothes, baggy slacks and a green T-shirt. Obviously, he wasn't going swimming because he hadn't brought a bathing suit. All he did was look at me and say, "I'm going to the gym, but I came here first to meet you."

I didn't answer.

"Why don't you come to the gym sometime and watch me work out?"

That was that. I was excited. I wasn't thinking romantically. Jake was married. And besides, I was sixteen and he was twenty-three. But this was Jake LaMotta, a famous fighter, the most famous fighter in the Bronx.

Jake trained at Gleason's Gym, which was two blocks from Joe's Meat Market. When I told my father, he liked the idea of watching Jake work out. "Come down, have lunch with me, and we'll go to the gym together," he said. So a few days later, I took the bus to Joe's, had lunch with my father, and then we went to see Jake.

I liked the gym. Maybe that's because I'm not from the fashionable upper east side of Manhattan. I grew up on the streets. When the workout ended, Jake told my father, "I'll drive Vikki home. You can trust me with her." That was good enough for Feebie. He went back to the meat market. Jake walked me to his car, a dark green Cadillac. I still wasn't thinking romantically because I knew he was married. And to make the point, the first question I asked was, "How's your wife?"

"We're not living together anymore," Jake told me. "She's staying with her mother."

That was all he said about it. Later, I learned they had a daughter who was a year old; that they'd gotten married eighteen months earlier, and Ida had moved out when Jake beat her. But I didn't see that side of him until much later. On that afternoon in May 1946, he treated me like a Dresden doll.

From then on, we saw each other almost every day. I'd go to school, Jake would go to the gym, and afterward we'd have dinner together, more often than not at his father's house. I felt comfortable with his family. His parents were divorced but I got to know them both. At first, his mother was cool to me, which was understandable. Jake was still married; Mama wanted a reconciliation, and I was only sixteen. But Papa welcomed me from the start. Meanwhile, my own father couldn't have been happier. Jake was a big name, and everyone in the neighborhood knew he was going out with Feebie's daughter.

Jake was my first boyfriend. Being with him made me feel safe. This was a time when I was having trouble with men and experiencing all sorts of problems. Now, here was a man who conjured up images of John Garfield. There was a sexual magnetism about him but he wasn't aggressive sexually. He treated me as though no one would ever hurt me again. He protected me completely.

Classes at school ended in June. During the summer, I saw Jake even more frequently than before. Every Sunday, I was invited with the rest of his family to Mama's extravaganza

Italian dinner. Then Jake's doberman pinscher had puppies and he gave me one from the litter. My father loved cigars. The best present you could give him was a good Havana. Jake bought him a whole box. But the nicest thing about being with Jake was that being with me seemed to make him happy. Whenever he saw me, his face seemed to light up. No matter where we were, his eyes were always on me. Everything we did together was comfortable and natural. It was only a matter of time before we grew intimate sexually.

The first time was at his father's apartment. We'd visited for dinner. Afterward, I did the dishes while Papa went to sleep. Then Jake and I talked for a while and went to lie down in the extra bedroom. We'd petted before but now we went further. Jake seemed to penetrate although he was shy about it, and I'm not sure he even penetrated completely. Then, a week later, we went to visit his mother, who was vacationing in upstate New York. Jake drove and, on the way back, a heavy rain left the roads unpassable. We stopped at a motel, and this time our love-making was complete. The only problem—and I didn't know it was a problem at the time—was that Jake used the withdrawal method of birth control.

"Don't worry," he told me. "You don't have to worry about anything because I'm pulling out."

And I didn't worry. I had complete trust in Jake.

Then in September I missed a period. And I was in a panic. What am I going to do? Legally, Jake was still married, and I didn't want to get married anyway.

The first thing I did was try every home remedy I'd ever heard about. We lived in a sixth floor apartment. For the next few weeks, whenever I went downstairs, I jumped the stairs instead of walking. Then I started taking hot baths with Epsom salts and running sprints on the streets because I'd heard that would help. Finally, I called Jake and said I had a problem. He picked me up in the Cadillac one afternoon after his workout, and I told him I'd missed my period.

"How late are you?"

"Two weeks."

"Let's wait and see. Maybe you'll still get it."

Then I missed October. And still not knowing what to do, I felt the only person who could help me was Jake. In truth, I wanted an abortion. Jake had told me once, he knew a doctor. I told myself, I'll put it in Jake's hands. He'll know how to handle this.

So again, I went to Jake. I told him I'd missed another period, and he began talking to himself in a herky-jerky pattern. "Well, I don't know. Ida's a problem . . . I could see my lawyer . . . No, not an abortion. That's no good."

And I wanted to shout, "Yes, an abortion." But abortion was a sin, and I wanted it to be Jake's sin, not mine. I wanted him to tell me to get an abortion because I was afraid to take the lead myself.

"I'll talk to my lawyer," Jake said. "I'll see what he can do."

Then, a few days later, Jake told me we were getting married. He'd spoken with his lawyer and was going to Mexico for a quickie divorce. I was a healthy clean girl; I'd be a good wife and mother; and he loved me. He was actually happy. "Vikki and a son. I want a son as much as I want the championship. What did I do to be so lucky!"

And I was sorry I'd told him. I said to myself, this is serious; I'm trapped. I don't want to get married. I'm sixteen years old. Maybe someday I'll marry Jake, but not now. I still want to play, go to dances, and hang out with my girlfriends.

Maybe if I'd had a friend who was older, or money of my own, or parents I could confide in, I'd have gotten the abortion. But those circumstances didn't exist; especially now that Jake knew I was carrying his "son." So instead, I dropped out of school and told my parents that Jake and I had decided to get married. Even then, I didn't tell them about being pregnant, although I think my mother suspected it. Maybe they thought marriage was the best thing for me. I don't know what they felt because they never told me. All I knew was, they didn't say what I wanted them to say: "Don't get married!"

Jake gave me a hundred dollars to buy a wedding outfit. I went shopping by myself, looking for something white, but bought a tan suit instead. Our wedding day was November 9, 1946. That morning, I dressed my hair in flowers and didn't say much. We were getting married in New Jersey because Mexican divorces weren't recognized by the New York courts. My mother and father were coming because I was underage, but no one else from either family had been invited. Early in the afternoon, Jake rang the doorbell to our apartment. My father looked out the window and shouted, "We'll be right down." Then I went into the bathroom, burst into tears, and started to vomit. I don't know how long I was in there; probably just a few minutes but it seemed like forever that I was crying and throwing up in the toilet. Finally, my mother opened the door, looked in, and said simply, "You know, it's not too late. You don't have to do this."

It's too late, I told myself. If you had come to me and said that last month or last week or even yesterday, maybe it would be different. But now? I'm dressed; Jake's waiting downstairs; I'm three months pregnant. It's too late.

Jake drove us to New Jersey. I sat in the front seat of the car. My parents were in back. As we rode through Manhattan, Jake pointed out the sights like we were tourists instead of native New Yorkers. "This is Central Park; this is the Empire State Building." When we got further south, it was, "This is the Staten Island Ferry." He was so happy.

The ceremony was conducted by a justice of the peace. Jake's lawyer, Irving Tell, was present. So was Irving's wife. Outside of my parents and the judge, that was it. When it was over, we drove back to New York. Jake dropped my parents off at the apartment and then we went to the house he'd bought for his mother. Mama lived on the ground floor; Jake on top. He carried me up a flight of stairs to the second floor and I began to panic. What am I doing here? Where am I?

Everything seemed strange. It was like a bad dream. Why am I in this man's bedroom? I was sixteen years old and had never been away from my parents in my life. I felt like a puppy that's been taken from its mother for the first time. I wanted to go home.

Some of Ida's belongings were still in the closet. It was as though I'd moved into someone else's house after she'd died. Jake began kissing me and taking my clothes off. Then we went to bed and, after we'd made love, I turned away so he wouldn't hear me and began to cry.

Chapter Five

Giacobe (Jake) LaMotta, the man I'd married, was born in New York on July 10, 1922. His father was a vegetable peddler; his mother a seamstress. When Jake was eight, the family moved to Philadelphia; but after being dispossessed from their apartment, they returned to the Bronx.

Jake was an unhappy boy, who became an unhappy man, who I'm convinced will be unhappy forever. His childhood was a perpetual struggle for survival. His father beat him. The atmosphere at home was devoid of love and caring. Every day, he fought just to get by.

As an adolescent, Jake committed a series of muggings and armed robberies. He was convicted three times on various charges and sentenced to the New York State reformatory for incorrigible youths at Coxsackie. Fighting came naturally. He wasn't articulate. He grew up surrounded by violence, at home and on the streets. He was part of that violence, and the violence was part of him.

Jake started boxing at age ten. In the neighborhood where he lived, grown men would construct rings bordered by crates on the street and solicit children to fight. They'd bet on the outcome and afterward, depending on how good the battle had been, throw coins to the winner. Jake loved it. He loved exerting his will, being in command, and showing his dominance by hurting an opponent. The ring was his home. There, life was simple. It was conquest and destruction, pure competition, man against man, the best man wins. Jack Dempsey, the legendary heavyweight champion, once said, "To be a good fighter, you have to have three things: you've got to be able to give it; you've got to be able to take it; and you've got to have a fighting heart." Jake had all three. In the ring, he knew who he was. And in the ring, he was able to escape the demons he was otherwise unable to control or understand.

When Jake and I got married, I didn't realize how deeply embedded his roots were in violence. I knew about his past as a delinquent, but on the surface at least, he seemed to regret it. I knew he was tough but I was used to that. I came from a tough neighborhood. One of the things about Jake that moved me the most was his reaction to a tragedy that had occurred before we met. Jake had been driving with his father when a boy ran from behind a tree onto the road and Jake's car hit him. They took the boy to Fordham Hospital but the doctors couldn't save him. He died, and for the next few months, Jake received crank calls and letters calling him a killer. He wasn't charged with any crime for the accident. He gave the entire purse from his next fight to the boy's family. But still, he was haunted by the death. It always bothered him. He was sensitive in that way, and protective of little people. Once we were married, I was his doll—his "pretty baby" he called me—and I thought he'd protect me forever.

After I got used to the idea of being away from my parents, our first year together was good. Both Jake and I came from large families. Brothers, sisters, and other relatives were always visiting. Jake was a surprisingly good cook and we hosted family dinners several nights a week. His father and I got along beautifully. I'm a good cook now, and a lot of what I learned came from Jake's father. Papa and I would go down to the piers early in the morning to collect fresh crabs and mussels off the rocks. He grew his own tomatoes in the backyard and taught me which grapes to buy at market for homemade wine. Whatever he did in the kitchen, whether it was making fresh pasta or baking bread, was done slowly with precision.

Meanwhile, Jake did things with me that I had always wanted to do but had never done with my father. Every Sunday, he'd take me to the movies, horseback riding, or to City Island. He taught me to drive a car and was a good teacher. During the winter, we'd walk in the snow for hours. He was the companion I'd never had in childhood. Something exciting always seemed to be happening. Every now and then, for no reason at all, he'd give me a hundred dollars. I was just starting to value good clothes, and a hundred dollars was a lot of money. Jake would hand me a paper bag with a hundred one-dollar bills in it and tell me to count them out loud while he watched.

I enjoyed our life. I was Jake's woman; a sixteen-year-old housewife, plain and simple. My place was at home; I never questioned what was happening. Women weren't supposed to learn a trade or go to college. That was considered a waste of time because the ultimate goal was to get married and have children. Jake and I would have children and grandchildren, and that would be my life forever.

Whatever Jake said governed. He was the boss; I was obedient. He dictated my thoughts, my opinions, and my values. I was there to serve him. We weren't partners. We never sat down and spoke in depth about what was happening.

The husband was in charge; that was how adults lived. If I thought differently about something, I was young, what did I know? I never considered what might please me; only what pleased Jake. I never thought about what I might want; only what Jake wanted. I wasn't unselfish; just ignorant. I didn't know any better, and Jake did everything in his power to perpetuate my ignorance.

People talk about Jake as being jealous—and he was—but it was more than that. He was all-consuming. He lived as part of me. If I went to visit my mother or father, Jake had to be there. If I wanted to speak with anyone, Jake was at my side. If I needed groceries, Jake wanted to go to the store with me. If the telephone rang, Jake had to answer it. I couldn't do anything unless he was there. Every aspect of my life was under his control.

"No! Don't go to the butcher without me. I'll be home from the gym early. We'll go together . . . What friends did you have over today? I don't like you seeing her unless I'm around." The hundred-dollar gifts in paper bags were nice but they came with a string attached. I had to spend the money in Jake's presence. And soon I learned that, if I needed money for food, clothes, or something for the house, the answer was, "You don't need money. We'll go out and I'll pay when we buy it together."

In the beginning, it was flattering. I told myself that Jake loved me and cared so much. Then I began to suffer the burden of being his possession. He was jealous of other men— I couldn't talk with the baker or grocer—but he didn't want me talking with other women either. Wherever I went, no matter what it was for, if it was with anyone besides his father, Jake had to be there.

No person can live like that. Part of life is being able to sit and talk and do things with someone other than a husband or wife. Years later, I asked Jake about his possessiveness: "Would you please tell me why you didn't allow me to visit my sisters alone? Why couldn't I have girlfriends in the house? Why did you have to be with me wherever I went?" And Jake's answer was simple: "I didn't want you to be with other people because I thought they'd put ideas in your head. I wanted to train you, so you only knew what I wanted you to know."

That was Jake. I was a possession, the prize he was afraid to let anyone touch. If a reporter came by for a newspaper or radio interview, Jake wanted me there to show off as his wife. But in real life, he wanted me tied down, as though he were afraid of losing me. In retrospect, I think he couldn't believe that someone as young and pretty and innocent as I was actually loved him. Still, at first, we were happy. Jake was a fighter on the rise, optimistic about his future, a celebrity in the Bronx. I was his good little girl, subservient and content. And our baby was coming.

Once Jake and I got married, being pregnant was a source of gratification. People kept giving me maternity clothes and showering attention on me. "How do you feel? How much weight have you gained lately?" I had the baby's room decorated and filled with dolls. I was like a child playing. Then I went to Westchester Square Hospital to give birth. I wasn't afraid; it was exciting.

At the hospital, they put me in a pre-delivery room with four other women. Every hour or so, a nurse would come in, examine me, and say, "The baby's not ready to come out yet." Otherwise, they were inattentive. After a while, I began to feel pain and the pain got worse, as though someone was sawing off the lower half of my body. Twice, I fell out of bed onto the floor and had to get back onto the bed myself. It lasted that way for eighteen hours. I didn't know what was happening or what to do. Jake and my parents weren't allowed in the room. I was alone, frightened, in horrible pain, without any reassurance. Finally, one of the nurses said, "The baby's coming," and they wheeled me to the delivery room. Then another nurse said, "The doctor's not here yet. Close her legs. We can't find the doctor." This after eighteen hours. So they closed my legs and held them shut. The baby was pushing, trying to come out, and two nurses were holding my legs together, waiting for the doctor. That went on for I don't know how long until the baby went back inside me. Then the doctor arrived and tried to induce labor but the baby wouldn't budge. Another hour went by and I heard them talking. They were afraid the baby was going to die. Finally, after twenty hours, Jack was born—on May 6, 1947—nine months after Jake and I had gone to bed together for the first time.

I liked being a mother. Jack was a good baby and my instincts were good. Growing up, I'd helped several neighbors with their children, so I knew what to do. The only problems I had were with Jake's mother. Whatever I did, she was always criticizing. In her time, babies' legs were bound to make them straight; so a baby would actually be lying in its bassinet with its legs tied together in a blanket. That seemed unnatural to me. I figured, let the legs grow the way they're supposed to grow. Mama had a fit. She also told me to wake the baby every four hours to feed him. I felt, if Jack was asleep, let him sleep.

I did most things on my own; some right and some wrong. At the time, formula was popular and I bottle-fed Jack. Jake's mother said I should breast-feed him and she was probably right. On the other hand, she had nursed her children until they were two years old, and I thought that was crazy. I took Jack off the bottle and began feeding him solid food as soon as he was old enough to eat.

Meanwhile, Jake was succeeding in the ring. As a fighter, he was in his prime; twenty-four years old, with sixty-four victories, many of them against leading contenders. Fighting Jake was like avoiding a lion in an eighteen-foot-square cage for ten rounds. And the tougher the opponent, the more he liked it.

Jake had eight fights in 1946, the year we were married. He won seven and fought a ten-round draw against Jimmy Edgar in Detroit. At the start of 1947, he won decisions over Tommy Bell and Tony Janiro to solidify his position as the top-ranked contender for the world middleweight championship. By then, he was a legend in the Bronx. Baseball and boxing were the only sports that mattered. Football didn't have much of a following and very few people followed basketball or hockey. Television was in its infancy and fight clubs were popular, so there was strong regional identification with fighters. Jake belonged to the Bronx the way the Dodgers belonged to Brooklyn. He was known as the Bronx Bull, not Raging Bull. Everywhere he went, people called his name. If we visited a nightclub, Cab Calloway or Billy Eckstein might ask us to join them at their table. And the money was starting to roll in. At the onset of his career, Jake had begun keeping a small paperback ledger. For each fight, he'd pencil in the date, opponent, result, and how much he'd earned. For his first fight, on March 3, 1941, he'd been paid twenty-five dollars. In his first ten bouts, he'd made a total of two hundred seventy-five dollars; fifty dollars for the second fight and twenty-five dollars for each of the others. In 1946, he made $88,520; an amount worth well over $500,000 in today's dollars.

Yet for all his success in the ring, Jake had two problems related to boxing. The first was his hands; they were small and brittle. His body was compact: five-feet-eight inches of power and muscle, but his hands betrayed him. After every fight, they were bruised and swollen. As ironic as it might sound, one of the reasons he attacked opponents' bodies as often as he did was the fear his hands couldn't withstand the constant pounding against other men's skulls.

The other problem was more formidable. Jake fought in an era when boxing was closely linked to organized crime. The underworld controlled boxing the way television and a few major promoters do today, and Jake wouldn't do business with the mob. He wouldn't listen to them; he wouldn't cooperate; he wouldn't socialize, be friendly, or do anything else they wanted. He refused to be involved with the underworld in any fashion. And the problem was, to fight for the championship, he needed a godfather. No matter how good he was in the ring, to get a title shot, he was going to have to do business with the powers that be.

He wouldn't do it. All Jake wanted was to be a champion. But he wanted it on his own terms, and that was impossible. Soon, he found himself relegated to the role of "policeman"— someone who fights all the tough fighters the champion is ducking. Those are the only big-money fights a policeman can get. Jake was beating the best fighters in the world, and still he couldn't get a title shot.

Jake's brother, Joey, lived across the street from us. Unlike Jake, Joey was very friendly with certain people in the mob. Time and again, he'd come to Jake and tell him that throwing a fight was the only road to the championship. Jake didn't want to hear it. The thing he was proudest of was being an honest fighter. But Joey was constantly in our living room, pushing, prodding. "Jake, you've got to do it. There's big money. You can win the title but first you've got to take a dive." Joey would bring hoods to the gym, and Jake would throw them out. Joey would plead with Jake to be more respectful to mob leaders and, if Jake met them on the street, he'd tell them to get lost.

Finally, Jake signed to fight Billy Fox at Madison Square Garden on November 14, 1947. Fox was a Philadelphia light-heavyweight with a record of forty-eight wins, one loss, and forty-eight knockouts. Jake was the pride of New York City, the number-one middleweight contender, and had never been knocked out in seventy-nine bouts.

A week before the fight, Jake got hurt. He was sparring in the gym, got hit, and suffered a bruised spleen. The pain was excruciating. His personal physician advised him to call the bout off. But before anyone could made a decision, Joey was there like a hawk. "Jake, now's the time. Throw the fight and you'll get a shot at the championship. You're hurt. Fox is a light-heavyweight. Even if you take a dive, nothing changes; you're still the number-one middleweight contender."

Jake didn't want to do it. Then, two days before the fight, Joey came back and said the mob had offered a title fight plus $100,000 in cash if Jake lost to Fox.

Jake never told me he threw the fight. Years later, when he testified before a Congressional subcommittee, I learned the truth. But in 1947, knowing how proud he was to be a fighter, I never dreamed he'd do it. Maybe I was naive; maybe I simply shut my eyes to what was going on around me. Regardless, Jake agreed to sell his soul to the devil.

All afternoon on the day of the fight, there were rumors of a fix. The odds, which had been even money, jumped to twelve to five in favor of Fox. Madison Square Garden was completely sold out with 18,340 fans in attendance. It was the fight of the year in New York. And it stank. Fox hit Jake with unanswered blows for four rounds but couldn't knock him down. Finally, the referee halted the bout; the first time in his career that Jake had been "knocked out."

Then all hell broke loose. The next morning, *The New York Times* declared, "The battle was attended by many strange developments, not the least of which was a flood of reports in advance that it would not be waged on its merits. LaMotta's fighting style, or lack of it, was another strange incident. The husky Bronx Italian, noted for his ability to inflict damage from a crouching style that makes him a difficult target for punching, a specialist in close-range fighting without a superior, fought up to expectations only in the first round."

The *Daily Mirror* called Jake's performance "feeble and mysterious" and stated, "LaMotta never fought as foolishly as he did last night. Every move he made might have been ordered by Fox. The art of pretending is one of the most difficult for an honest fighter to master. Jake's first local appearance as a thespian was redolent of Westphalian ham."

The *New York Post* graded Jake's ring effort "thoroughly unsatisfactory" and proclaimed, "LaMotta seemingly asked for it as early as the second round, when he stuck his chin out and invited Fox to hit it."

And there was more. The *Journal American*: "I wouldn't swear that I saw prearrangement in the knockout that Billy Fox scored over Jake LaMotta. I will say that, from any standpoint, it was the most questionable looking fight I've seen in the Garden."

The *Daily News:* "He was a poor actor, slamming away with mock ferocity in the first round at Fox's body. This naturally invited shots by Fox at LaMotta's open jaw. LaMotta is not that much of a raw amateur."

And the *World Telegram*: "Somebody got rich on this biggest fight of the year, even though the bookmakers knocked it off the boards at mid-afternoon."

Jake had lost fights before. I'm sure he thought Billy Fox would be just another loss; that he could throw the fight quietly, pick up an IOU from the mob, and go on to challenge for the world middleweight championship. But it had been too obvious. Responding to the headlines and cries of scandal, the New York State Athletic Commission withheld Jake's purse and began an investigation of the fight. A second inquiry was launched by the New York County District Attorney's office. Not only had Jake gone against his principles; he was publicly disgraced, his reputation as a fighter ruined. All his life, he'd wanted to be admired for his skill in the ring. He didn't care what people thought about him personally. His integrity as a fighter was what mattered. Now that had been destroyed.

What hurt most were our neighbors; people who worked hard for their money, who had bet on him and lost. Before each fight, Jake would walk down the street. People would come up and ask, "You gonna win?" and he'd answer, "Yeah, put your money on me." People had known he was an honest fighter; that they could bet on him and he'd do his best. Now that was gone. He was "Jake the Fake", an object of mistrust and scorn. He had betrayed them.

Three months after the Fox fight, the New York State Athletic Commission concluded its investigation. Because there was no conclusive proof of a fix, Jake was awarded his purse. However, he was fined $1,000 and suspended for seven months for "deliberately concealing and failing to report an injury"—the hematoma on his spleen. That left him more depressed than ever. First, he'd lost his pride. Now, he couldn't do what he defined himself by, which was fight.

The next seven months were among the worst of Jake's life. He stayed indoors, alone, and wouldn't talk to anybody. He refused to go out because he was ashamed to be seen on the streets. He didn't train because there was nothing to train for. He was a changed person, horribly depressed and unhappy with life.

Only one thing kept him alive. If and when he fought again, the mob owed him a title shot.

Chapter Six

While Jake was suspended, life went on. In January 1948, I became pregnant with a second child. This time, I got a different doctor and avoided Westchester Square Hospital. On October 11th, Joey was born. Jack had been a quiet baby, happy and easy to care for. Joey was an infant maniac, but that happens sometimes.

Meanwhile, Jake's depression deepened but he was unwilling to discuss his problems. Verbal communication wasn't his style. Our conversations had always been, let's have dinner, let's go to this movie. We never talked about the emotions and relationships that shaped our lives. Neither of us knew how. Then, in the midst of Jake's depression, an incident occurred that underscored how little we really talked to each other.

Growing up in the Bronx, Jake had been friends with Rocky Graziano. Later, they'd served time together at the Coxsackie reformatory and turned to professional boxing at the same time. Within the trade, Rocky was extremely well-connected. Because of those connections, he'd gotten two shots at the world middleweight championship while Jake was still a contender. One afternoon when I was home with Jake, his brother Joey, and the children, Rocky came to visit. And who was he with? The man who had raped me three years earlier—Sal.

I had tried to tell Jake about the rape before we were married; that it had happened and there was nothing I could do about it. But he'd changed the subject as though I wasn't even talking and pushed it aside. He didn't want to know. Now Sal was standing in our kitchen, as cocky and arrogant as ever, looking at me as though nothing had happened, smiling and saying hello. He knew who I was. Probably, he knew before he set foot in the house because Jake and I had our pictures in the newspapers fairly often. First, I got angry—the nerve of this man, coming into Jake's home! Then I got scared. I pulled Jake's brother, Joey, into the bedroom, told him who Sal was, and Joey said he'd handle everything: "Don't panic. Stay here. I'll take care of it." Which Joey did, by doing nothing. Rocky and Sal left soon after, and nobody told Jake anything. I never told Jake who Sal was.

Later, I asked Rocky about Sal. He told me that Sal was a strong-arm man for the mob. They had low-level punks, middle-level, and top-of-the-line operatives. Sal was in the middle. He chauffeured the bigs, broke a few legs, things like that. I'd been right in fearing what might have happened if I'd gone to the police after he raped me.

Sal is dead now. Years later, when I was in my thirties, the police discovered his body in the trunk of a car with six bullets in his head. He lived like a hood and he died like one.

Jake's suspension from the ring was lifted by the New York State Athletic Commission in June of 1948. Right away, he wanted to fight for the title, but again there were problems. The fallout from his loss to Billy Fox was too great. Everyone knew he'd taken a dive and his image had to be rehabilitated before he could challenge for the crown. Over the next three months, he knocked out Ken Stribling, Burl Charity, and Johnny Colan. Then he won ten-round decisions over Vern Lester and Tommy Yarosz. Four more bouts followed in early 1949. Finally, Joey came back with word from the mob. Jake would be allowed to fight Marcel Cerdan of France for the world middleweight championship—with one hitch. Jake's purse would be $19,000. And to get the fight, he'd have to pay $20,000 in cash. In other words, he'd be fighting for nothing except the opportunity to win the title.

Jake didn't have the money. His $100,000 bribe from the Fox fight had been invested in a parking lot in the Bronx. His legitimate earnings had gone for living expenses, taxes, and family expenditures. All we had was $10,000 in the bank. I gave him my engagement ring to hock, then the rest of my jewelry. Finally, we gathered $20,000. Jake gave it to Joey and the date was set—Jake LaMotta versus Marcel Cerdan for the world middleweight championship, June 16, 1949, at Briggs Stadium in Detroit.

I'd never been to one of Jake's fights before. After we met, I listened to them on radio with my parents. Sometimes the tension was so great that I'd have to go outside and walk the streets until the fight was over. Then, after we were married, I'd travel to the fight site and stay at the hotel without going to the arena.

The morning of the Cerdan fight, Jake sat me down in our hotel suite and said, "I want you at ringside. You have to be there. I've waited my entire life for this." He was very calm, not at all nervous. He was waiting for Cerdan with the same anticipation that a child has waiting for Christmas. "There's no chance I'll be hurt. I'm going to win."

So I went to the fight. And it was a thing of beauty to watch. Jake had been born to win the middleweight championship of the world, and that night he was overpowering. Early in the bout, Cerdan tore a muscle in his left shoulder. The injury robbed him of his jab and left hook; it was painful and disabling. From then on, Jake was in complete command, hitting and not getting hit, totally dominating his foe. But even if Cerdan hadn't been hurt, I'm convinced that Jake would have won. His attitude, his conditioning, everything about him was perfect that night. His entire life had been aimed toward that moment. The bout was stopped by the referee when Cerdan was unable to answer the bell for the tenth round. Jake was middleweight champion of the world.

That night, in our hotel room, we drank champagne. Jake was exhausted, lying on the bed while I put cold compresses against his face. Then, while he soaked his hands in ice water, I went into the bathroom to take a bath. He was half-asleep when I came back out. I wanted to excite him and I was wearing what I'd planned: white silk stockings, a white string bikini, and the championship belt. That was Jake's moment. He was at the summit with the woman and the title of his dreams.

In the morning, I was branded with belt marks all over my body. The *Detroit Times* devoted five full pages to the fight including a headline that ran across the entire front page and read simply, "LaMotta Wins." The *New York Journal American* carried a red-type headline on page one. When we returned to the Bronx, the entire neighborhood was cordoned off. Streets were shut down. There were balloons and banners. Jake and I stood in the middle of the block outside our home, and over and over he kept saying, "I'm the champ." He deserved it. He was the best middleweight in the world. And then, midway through the celebration, he turned sullen. "I'm the champ," he said again. "But look what I had to do to get it."

That was the problem. Jake had sold his soul. The title was tainted. It was a dirty championship because of the Billy Fox fight. I honestly believe Jake felt inside that, once he was champion, the sun would shine every day, he'd be happy all the time, and life would be perfect. But the world doesn't work that way and, having won the title, he was still depressed without knowing why. More and more, he sought to bolster his ego by being loud and obnoxious. "Have no fear; the champ is here," he'd tell people. If I disagreed with him about anything, all I heard was, "Don't answer the champ back. Nobody talks back to the champ."

Once, we ran into the comedian, Fat Jack Leonard, on the street in front of Lindy's Restaurant. He and Jake knew each other as celebrities. Jack was the sort of person who, the minute he sees you, he starts telling jokes. He told us one and Jake punched him in the stomach. Leonard doubled over. Jake looked at him and said, "What did you expect? You make your living telling jokes. I'm the champ. That's how I make mine."

He started going out more at night. One thing would lead to another and someone would say, "Come on, champ. Let me buy you a drink." I didn't drink. Except for celebrations, my standard fare was Coca Cola with a shot glass full of maraschino cherries on the side. Jake was the same way. But after he won the title; well, he was the champ. Why not have a drink? And then another, which is death for a fighter. Soon, he was losing the motivation to train. "I'm not doing road-work today. Instead of running, I'll spar an extra round in the gym." He wasn't hungry anymore. The edge was gone. And as he began to slip as a fighter, another problem returned to the fore.

Jake had always been jealous. Part of that derived from the fact that he wasn't a sexual person. He was gentle as a lover; but our lovemaking was infrequent and always for a very short time, as though he felt it was something he ought to do. Then he'd go into training and, for five or six weeks, we'd have no sex at all. I didn't mind the abstinence. Maybe men are different from women in that respect; I don't know. But as far as I was concerned, Jake was my man. I wasn't interested in sleeping with anyone else. If I had to wait six weeks to make love, fine. We'd be in training together. But I don't think Jake felt secure in my love. He couldn't believe I had no interest in other men. Once, when he was supposed to be away at training camp preparing for a fight, he came home unannounced and I thought he was insane. "Vikki, you've been cheating on me . . . Don't lie; I know it's true. My brother Al heard you on the phone, talking love talk to some guy . . . Don't lie. I told Al to keep an eye on you. He told me everything you said." Then Jake proceeded to repeat every word Al had overheard me saying to my lover. And when he finished, I looked at him and said, "Jake, think! That was yesterday. I was on the phone with you."

Another time, when Jake was out of town, my brother Don came to the house so I wouldn't be alone. He spent the night and, in the morning, went to work. Al told Jake that I'd had a guy sleeping over while he was gone. Can you imagine? With Jake's mother living downstairs, would I be crazy enough to sleep with another man one flight above? But Jake didn't believe me. He went to Don and questioned him on every detail.

So there was a problem with jealousy, and always had been. Then, after Jake won the title, I began to get more attention than before. Newspapers and magazines were running my picture. Photographers' cameras followed me at ringside. I got fan mail, sometimes more than Jake, and he didn't like it. He became more possessive than ever. The whole idea of my having an affair was absurd. I loved Jake. And even if I hadn't, I would never have given another man the opportunity to look down on him. Jake was my husband, the father of our children. But he didn't see it that way; and as his jealousy grew, everything else around him was falling down.

In October 1949, while flying to New York for a rematch with Jake, Marcel Cerdan was killed in a plane crash. The tragedy left forever unresolved the question of how they would have fared against one another in their first fight had Cerdan not injured his shoulder. Meanwhile, the public was turning against Jake with ferocity and venom. The 1940s were a time for myths. Few people saw the men behind the image of America's sports heroes. But in Jake's case, because of the Billy Fox fight, the man was known. And beyond that, Jake made no effort to hide his darker side. Soon after he won the title, *Newsweek* called him "more hated than any two other boxing champions." W.C. Heinz, one of the most respected writers of that era, penned an article entitled "The Host Hated Man In Sports" and closed with the words "Jacob LaMotta will go into the books as one of the most unpopular figures of all time."

It was bad. And worse, Jake couldn't rid himself of the mob. They'd provided him with his title shot. They still had Billy Fox to hold over him. And now that Jake was champion, the mob dictated who his opponents would be. Tiberio Mitri in New York. Laurent Dauthuille in Detroit. And finally, Sugar Ray Robinson in Chicago.

There have been very few truly great rivalries in boxing. Muhammad Ali and Joe Frazier, Jack Dempsey and Gene

Tunney, Willie Pep and Sandy Sadler are among the ones that come to mind. Such rivalries are rare because great fighters seldom cross paths in the ring; and when they do, once is usually enough for both men.

Pound for pound, Sugar Ray Robinson might have been the greatest fighter of all time. Most boxers can hurt an opponent with a straight right, an uppercut, or hook, but not with all three punches. Most fighters can disable a foe with the first or last punch in a combination, but not with every punch in a sequence. Robinson could knock an opponent out with any punch at any time. In his first 131 professional fights, he lost once. That was to Jake on a ten-round decision in 1943. From October 1942 through September 1945, Jake and Ray fought each other five times. Robinson won four of those encounters but was never able to knock Jake down.

Sugar Ray Robinson won the world welterweight championship in 1946 and successfully defended his title five times. Then he began looking for higher mountains to climb. Fighting Jake for the middleweight title was the obvious move. It was a fight everyone wanted. Robinson, because he thought Jake was slipping as a fighter. Jake, because he loved the challenge of going against the best in the world. The public, because their previous battles had been filled with drama. And the mob, because Jake had become an embarrassment and hence a liability. They wanted him to lose.

The bout was scheduled for Valentine's Day, February 14, 1951 at Chicago Stadium. On January 1st, when Jake went into final training, he weighed 177 pounds. That meant, in addition to normal pre-fight preparation, he had to lose seventeen pounds in six weeks or forfeit his title on the scales. It was a difficult task under the best of circumstances. And for Jake, there was an added problem. After he won the championship, he'd been approached by a doctor who'd told him, "I have an injection from Italy made from the pollinas of a bull. You know how strong you are now? If you take these injections, you'll be fifty times stronger."

Jake heard this—the pollinas of a bull; stronger than I am now—and right away, he was taking the shots. One time, he overdosed. His face turned blue; his feet were like ice. But he wouldn't terminate the injections; and of course, what he was putting into his body was a precursor of today's steroids.

Throughout his career, Jake had always had difficulty "making weight." Once he started taking the injections, the problem grew worse. At one point, I read a newspaper article which said there were new substances called synthetic hormones that might cause cancer. I was worried and went to another doctor for information. The doctor told me that these hormones were new. No one was sure exactly what they did, but one thing was certain; they caused a person to gain weight and become bloated with water.

Jake wouldn't listen. I went home and told him what I'd learned; how the hormones were blowing him up with excess water. "What do you know about boxing?" he demanded. "I'm the champ. You mind your own business; I'll take care of the fighting."

A month before the Robinson fight, Jake managed to get his weight down to 168 pounds; eight pounds over the middleweight limit. Then he went on a four-day fast, but couldn't get below 164. For the next four weeks, he limited himself to 1,500 calories a day and trained on Benzedrine to make up for the strength he lost from not eating. He all but killed himself trying to make weight. Sometimes, he'd buy a huge piece of steak, boil it for hours, and drink the water as beef soup. Relatively little was known about nutrition in those days. But even then, it was obvious that cooking beef that way took the nourishment out of it. "I'm the champ. What do you know about nutrition? Keep your mouth shut."

The evening before the fight, Jake weighed 164-1/2 pounds. He spent the night in a steam room before weighing in at 160. There was no way he could win. How could a man fight after barely eating solid food for four weeks? He belonged in a hospital.

On the night of the fight, thirty million people—one-fifth the population of the United States—watched Jake and Sugar Ray Robinson on television. Robinson was a 17-to-5 favorite; partly because he had won four of their five previous bouts and partly because he was a fighter on the rise while Jake was on the way down. Eight years had passed since their fight in Detroit, when Jake had knocked Sugar Ray through the ropes en route to the only loss in the first eleven years of Robinson's career.

The bell for round one sounded. Jake and Sugar Ray Robinson were alone in the ring with the eyes of the nation upon them. Robinson was the better fighter; everyone knew that. But Jake had the style to beat him. For eight rounds, Sugar Ray dazzled the crowd with his speed and footwork; a brilliant presence virtually floating in the ring. And for eight rounds, Jake trudged forward, forcing the fight, battling from a low coiled crouch as the bull and the matador fought on even terms. Then, in the ninth round, the fight changed. Whatever strength and stamina Jake had brought into the ring were gone. And it was then that all his mistakes came back to haunt him. The mornings he hadn't run; the days he'd eased up in the gym; the times he'd been lazy, stayed up too late, or had a drink with the boys. For eight rounds, he'd given his best. Now he had nothing left and Robinson was still strong.

Over the next four rounds, Jake was battered as brutally as any man has ever been battered in the ring. All the punches he'd taken in his life wouldn't add up to the beating he sustained that night. His eyes were puffed; he was bleeding badly, staggering blindly. His championship was gone but he wouldn't go down. I sat there, screaming, crying, and ultimately praying, "Let it be over. Please! Let it end."

Jake wouldn't fall. All he had left was pride in never having been knocked off his feet. Not by Billy Fox, not by Sugar Ray Robinson, not by anyone. Not ever, and not now. Finally, in the thirteenth round with Jake draped helplessly against the ropes, the referee intervened. Sugar Ray Robinson was the new middleweight champion. Jake was deposed, but he hadn't gone down.

After the fight, I went into the dressing room. Jake was stretched out on a table, semi-conscious with oxygen being administered to him. Blood was flowing from his nose and mouth. His face had been torn apart so badly it looked as though it might never be pieced together again. His lips and eyes were horribly swollen. I thought he was dying.

"I never went down," he whispered. That's all he could say. "I never went down."

But his career as a fighter was shattered. Physically and psychologically, Sugar Ray Robinson had destroyed him. Jake was never the same in or out of the ring again.

Chapter Seven

After Jake lost his title to Sugar Ray Robinson, the sporting press seemed willing to forgive past sins and rally to his side. Given the beating he'd taken, it would have been hard to do otherwise.

Dan Parker, whose columns had savaged Jake after the Billy Fox fight, took the lead, writing in the *New York Daily Mirror*, "Jake LaMotta wasn't much as middleweight champion until the last few minutes of his reign. Then he atoned for everything. Beaten to a bloody pulp by Ray Robinson, half-blind with his title beyond hope of salvaging, Jake had one precious possession left and nothing but fierce pride to defend it with. As the thirteenth round of their Chicago Stadium battle opened, no one had ever knocked him off his feet. Through two agonizing minutes, Jake braced himself and helplessly took everything Robinson fired at him with fortitude that made the early Spartans seem cowardly."

Other writers followed suit. Ray Robinson called Jake "the toughest fighter of the era." Not just the toughest fighter Robinson had faced, but the toughest of his time.

The moment was right for Jake to retire. His strength was

gone. He'd lost the will a fighter needs to compete. His body no longer responded to the demands of his trade. One week after the Robinson bout, his weight ballooned to 187 pounds. But boxing was all Jake knew. It was his livelihood and also his way of living. Four months after the loss to Robinson, he fought again and, still on his feet, was knocked out by Bob Murphy in the seventh round. Seven months later, he lost for the third time in a row, on a ten-round decision to Norman Hayes.

He began to brood more than ever, feeling desperate without knowing why. His drinking increased and jealousy turned to paranoia. Looking back, I think Jake was a basically insecure man who needed me to prove his masculinity. Possessing what he thought was a dazzling sex object enabled him to feel better about himself. But once his status as a world-class fighter evaporated, he felt as though he had nothing to bind me. His fear was that I'd been in love with Jake LaMotta the famous boxer, not Jake the man. He was afraid of losing me and every social situation became a crisis.

Jake and I would go out for dinner, and there'd be another couple sitting nearby. Afterward, we'd come home and Jake would say, "Did you notice that guy at the next table?" I'd say no, and Jake would tell me, "He was a good-looking guy. You didn't notice? I thought he was looking at you." Either way, I was damned. If I said, "Yes, I noticed," then I was looking for an affair. If I said no, then I was hiding something. It got to the point where, if we were walking on the street and a man passed, I'd have to avert my eyes. And with any man who came into my life in the most tangential way—a salesman, a guest at someone's house where we went for dinner—we'd come home and Jake would start. "He was a good-looking guy, wasn't he? You probably thought he was good-looking. Boy, did you see the way he noticed you tonight? You wouldn't go out with somebody like that, would you? I mean, what if he put the moves on you?"

The situation was intolerable.

Jake was constantly worried. And no matter what I said, it was wrong. There was no way to convince him I wasn't going to have an affair. His paranoia was out of control, and the best way to explain it is to tell you how he remodeled our home. He took a ground-floor room and turned it into a supermarket. There were salamis and cheeses hanging from the ceiling, a freezer full of meat, and shelves loaded with everything from toilet paper to spaghetti. If I needed more meat, he'd tell me, "Don't go out; I'll get it from my cousin the butcher, Charlie Petrillo." If we needed canned goods it was, "Stay here. I'll have a carload delivered." So now I didn't have to go shopping, did I? All I had to do was walk downstairs into my own little store. I was a prisoner in my own home.

And still, Jake's jealousy knew no bounds. My parents had a pass to a new swimming pool in the Bronx. I'd go there occasionally with the children. We'd sit with my parents, brothers and sisters, and talk. Everybody who went to the pool knew each other. The people were friendly. That's the way it was. One evening, during a family dinner, my sister Pat mentioned that there was a good-looking guy who went to the pool. Jake's ears perked up. "How old is this guy?"

"About your age," my mother told him. "And so handsome; he looks like Tony Curtis. I think I'm in love."

That was all Jake needed to hear. As soon as my parents left, he started. "You're going out with this guy. You've been hiding him from me, Vikki." And I told him, "Jake, that's ridiculous. He's just a guy who goes to the pool."

"Well, I'm going to the pool tomorrow," Jake announced.

The following day at noon, he took the car and drove me to Shorehaven Pool. I was dying, wondering what was going to happen. We got there, and Jake led me to an area where my view of the water was blocked by a row of shrubs. "Stay here," he ordered. "I'll be back in a minute." Then he left, and all I could do was sit and pray, "Please, God, don't let him embarrass me or hurt anybody."

A few minutes later, Jake came back, happy as a lark. "Come on, Vikki. Let's go home." In the car, I asked what had happened and he wouldn't tell me. All he said was, "I taught him a lesson." That night, my sister Pat gave me a full report. Jake's not a talker or a yeller. He just does what he wants to do. He'd gone up to the guy and didn't say anything; just punched him in the stomach. The guy doubled over and Jake told him, "Stay away from my wife." And of course, that gave Jake exactly what he wanted. I was too embarrassed to go back to the pool again.

But now something else was going on. When Jake and I got married, I'd been obedient and docile. I was a child bride and had acted like a child, waiting to be told what to think and what to do. Anytime I dared question his views, it was, "Shut your mouth; what do you know." And God forbid I should display any talent. That was the last thing in the world Jake wanted.

From time to time, I'd try to draw; charcoal sketches of fruit, flowers, or faces. I'd take a picture of Louis Armstrong or someone else out of a magazine and recreate it as best I could. Jake was always critical of my work. "You're copying," he'd say. "That's not art. All you're doing is copying the pictures." Eventually, I limited my drawing to times when he was out of the house because I was embarrassed by his comments. Then one day, he came home while I was sketching. "Oh, look!

Vikki's copying again. That's not art. Why don't you just cut some pictures out of a magazine and frame them." I answered back and Jake grabbed my sketches—not just the one I was working on; all of them—and ripped them to pieces. "Now they're really garbage," he told me.

But things were changing. Jake's loss of his title and his decline as a fighter were coinciding with my emergence as a woman. I was now twenty-one years old and growing more assertive, starting to say, "Hey, wait a minute; I have ideas of my own." I wasn't willing to accept Jake's views as absolute anymore.

Jake had liked it when I did what he told me to do. He didn't like it when I began to think for myself. And for the first time in our marriage, he began to get physically abusive. There had been previous hints of violence. Once, a year after we'd gotten married, I'd been sitting at the kitchen table with Jake and my sister Pat. We were talking and I said something— I don't remember what—that Jake didn't like. Up until then, he'd been very gentle with me. But this time, he got angry and reached out with the back of his hand to slap me. The blow caught the bridge of my nose and pushed it to the side of my face. I started bleeding, choking on the blood. Jake was crying; he couldn't believe what he'd done. He pushed my head back, snapped the bone into place, and drove me to a doctor. It was winter, very cold out. The doctor examined my nose and, when we left his office, there was a huge man standing just outside, dressed in a peak cap and tan cashmere coat. I don't impress easily, but this man's presence was extraordinary. Then Jake said, "Hi, Babe," and I realized it was Babe Ruth. And of course, Ruth was a big boxing fan, so he recognized Jake. They talked for quite a while. Ruth said he was going to the same doctor. He was very nice, smiling, and seemed happy. It wasn't until later that we learned he was being treated for throat cancer, which eventually killed him.

So that was my first physical incident with Jake. It had a happy ending because I met Babe Ruth. And it was an accident. Then, a few years later, Jake and I were kidding around, play-boxing one night. He was punching and I was blocking. I saw an opening; you learn a person's moves if you do it long enough. And I whacked him. Jake didn't expect it. He was off-balance and sort of fell back. I started laughing, and he hit me—hard, on the arm. He hit me to hurt me, and then he said, "That'll teach you to hit the champ."

I never play-boxed with Jake again, and I learned to stay out of his way when he was angry. But after the loss to Robinson, he became more aggressive physically. He'd push me around, shove me, twist my arm in a way that let me know I shouldn't resist because, if I did, he'd hurt me. There weren't any beatings; not yet anyway. But there was physical intimidation that hadn't existed between us before. I began to ask, "Why am I with someone who's treating me this way?" I didn't like it.

Then Jake, the jealous one, started going out nights. Not often at first, but it was still unusual because for years he'd stayed home virtually every evening. "I'm going out with the boys," he'd tell me. Soon he was coming home late, smelling of whiskey and perfume with lipstick all over his shirt. That was new to me. I'd never experienced sexual infidelity before. Cheating hadn't been part of my upbringing. I'm quite sure my father, for all his faults, was sexually faithful to my mother. And the reason I say that is, as a child, I'd spent a lot of time with the men at Harry's Bar and Grill. I'd hear them talking about who was fooling around and who had slept with who. I'd see men with different women and notice

how they acted. I'd learned to recognize the deception in their
eyes, and I'd never seen my father that way. I never saw him
flirt or even look at another woman. All he cared about was
my mother and cards. But now, Jake was playing around. It was
obvious. I got mad. I didn't like what I was seeing. I was hurt
and upset and starting to lose it for Jake. I stayed faithful; but
more and more, I was becoming emotionally detached.

Then, one night when Jake was out, my sister Phyllis and
I went to the Pelham Heath Inn for a drink. We walked into
the lounge, and the first person I saw was Jake, sitting in back
with a woman, having a drink. He saw us and an agitated look
crossed his face. If the situation was innocent, he'd have reacted
differently, invited us to join him, but his face said something
else. He'd been caught. Phyllis and I turned and walked out to
the street.

Neither of us realized it but Jake was following. Just as we
reached Pelham Parkway, he shoved me from behind, practically knocking me into an oncoming bus. He didn't say a
word, not during the entire incident. I regained my balance
and ran. And then, for the first time in my life, I went to my
parents because I was afraid of Jake. I'd seen the meanness and
violence in his make-up, and it frightened me. Thank God for
my father; he'd protect me.

They were both home, Margie and Feebie. I told them
what had happened and said, "I'm afraid, please let me stay
here tonight." And my mother answered, "You made your bed.
Now you lie in it."

She was the ruler; my father didn't say a word. Later in
the evening, Jake came to pick me up, smiling as though
nothing had happened, and we went home together. Then, a
month later, I learned I was pregnant again. I knew we had
problems, which is putting it mildly. It was hard to tolerate

what was happening between us. But I wanted the child and, on March 25, 1952, our daughter Chris was born.

Meanwhile, Jake kept fighting. I wanted him to retire, but he wouldn't quit. On March 5, 1952, he fought a ten-round draw against Eugene Hairston; his fourth bout in a row without a victory. Several months later, he avenged the draw as well as earlier losses to Norman Hayes and Bob Murphy with ten-round decisions over each fighter. I admired Jake's courage in stepping into the ring, day after day, week after week. There's no harder, more demanding job than being a boxer, but there was no longer any point to it. His career was over. As a fighter he was shot.

Then, out of nowhere, Jake began talking about moving to Miami. We'd been to Florida several times. Both of us loved the beach and ocean. Jake knew several people who lived in Florida and they all said it was an ideal place to raise children.

I didn't want to go. New York was my home. I was a New York girl; I loved New York. But by then I was desperate. Jake was drinking, womanizing, and losing his grip on life. I couldn't stand to see the man I'd married, who had once been a superb athlete, acting loud and obnoxious, lurching into rooms, shouting, "Have no fear, the champ is here." I was willing to do almost anything to save our marriage. Let's try it, I decided. Our life together was going nowhere. Maybe in Miami, we'd find something more.

I remember sitting in the living room of our house in New York as the movers carried our possessions out to the van. It was a funny feeling, similar to the one I'd had six years earlier when Jake and I had gotten married.

If I'd known what lay ahead for us in Florida, I never would have gone.

Chapter Eight

Miami assaulted the senses. It was an explosion of color; green grass and blue water contrasting with houses that were red, pink and orange. At first, I was lonely. Leaving New York meant saying good-bye to friends and relatives; but after a while, I was too busy to mind. We bought a house in Miami Beach for $35,000. The LaGorse Golf Course bordered our property and was a wonderful playground for Jack and Joey, who loved building castles in the sandtraps and putting oranges in golf holes.

Jake very quickly became a celebrity about town. One of the things I'd liked about him when we met was that he'd seemed quiet and shy. Now, I realized, he needed attention. And since his career was fading, the only way he could get it was by being flamboyant and loud. Soon everyone in Miami Beach knew his Cadillac, wild shirts, and cigars. He was offensive at times; dense, poignant, and even funny at others.

One afternoon, he came home with a trumpet. "They're easy to play," he told me. Now keep in mind, this was the former middleweight champion of the world; the Bronx Bull, strong. He picked up the trumpet, puffed up his cheeks, stuck his chest out, and blew. Nothing happened. So he did it again, and again there was no sound. Jake's face turned red. He couldn't believe it. He didn't understand what was wrong. I told him, "Jake, you can't just blow. You have to learn how." And he got mad: "What do you know? I'll do it my way. I know how."

But comical moments were few and far between. Jake's jealousy was as bad as ever. More and more, he sought to intimidate me physically. And as the children grew older, they were becoming another source of conflict between us.

Jake had been a good father when Jack and Joey were infants. He'd loved being around them and was capable of playing "coochie-coo" for hours. But people have different strengths and weaknesses as parents. Some are very good until their children are a year old. Then they can't handle a toddler who's starting to walk, break things, and throw food. Others have difficulty caring for infants but are ideal with children learning to explore and do things on their own. Jake was a wonderful parent as long as he could tell the kids what to do and they did it. But he had trouble dealing with them as they developed minds of their own. Meanwhile, all around him, things seemed to be tumbling down. And as the year progressed, even he had to admit that his career as a fighter was just about over. Part of the problem was that he'd lost the desire to train. Partly, it was that too many ring wars had taken their toll. Most damaging though, his drinking had spiraled completely out of control.

Jake knew what was happening. Throughout 1952, he kept a diary with penciled notations indicating how he'd trained in the gym, his weight, and whether the day had been "good" or "bad." As the months passed, his degeneration was catalogued on diary pages written in his own hand. "Alcohol seems to stay in your system and doesn't want to come out"..."Drank too much and got sick"..."Ate bad and drank bad"..."Black Friday—drank all day"... "Rested all day, ate bad, drank bad. Gained eight pounds in one day"..."Drank bad".... "Drank bad"....

Finally, on New Year's Eve, Jake was knocked out in the eighth round of a bout in Coral Gables, Florida, by a club fighter named Danny Nardico. For the first time in his career, he was actually knocked down. "Lost by KO in 7," he wrote that night in his diary. "Went down for the first time in my life. Felt like I had no pep and no strength in my arms. Maybe it was my diet. I wasn't eating too much and could not train too hard. It could be this summer I had a very bad summer. Or maybe I'm just washed up."

Whatever the reasons, Jake was through as a fighter. And as 1953 began, he was forced to think about what he'd do for a career after boxing. His first decision was a bad one. Right after the Billy Fox fight, he'd bought a large piece of property across the street from Yankee Stadium in the Bronx. It was a corner lot. On days and nights when the stadium was in use, it yielded top dollars from concessionaires and parking. Other times, he promoted local boxing matches there himself. It was a good investment; our "annuity for life" Jake had called it. Then, in 1953, his brother Joey came down to Miami and talked him into selling the lot to a friend. Jake got some cash, although not as much as the land was worth. It was the story of his life. He'd do something brilliant like buying a great piece of property, and then blow it by doing something wrong.

So Jake wasn't fighting; his "annuity" was gone; our savings were dwindling; and still he wouldn't get a job. Then in October, he had his first brush with Miami law enforcement authorities. According to a crippled shoeshine man named

Jimmy Psaltides, Jake sat down at his stand and refused to get a shine. "I wasn't making any money," Psaltides told the police, "so I asked him to leave and he slugged me."

Jake was charged with assault and battery and freed on $1,000 bond. Faced with the threat of criminal prosecution, he paid Psaltides $1,500 to settle the matter and charges were dropped. Soon afterward, out of desperation, he returned to the ring but just didn't have it anymore. Finally, in April 1954, he retired for good after a ten-round loss to a club fighter named Billy Kilgore who wouldn't have lasted two minutes against Jake in his prime.

So there we were. I knew Jake had problems. I knew he couldn't handle certain things. I wanted to help, but didn't know how. Psychiatric counseling wasn't an option for people like us at the time. I wasn't allowed to say, "Hey, Jake, I think maybe this is what we should do" or "why don't we consider such and such." All I could do was hope for the best and look to the last real hope on our horizon.

Soon after Jake and I had gotten to Miami, he'd begun looking for a business and found a wonderful site for a bar. The building was located on the corner of Collins Avenue and 23rd Street, directly across from the Roney-Plaza Hotel. Jake had spent $100,000 remodeling the structure, dividing it into a cocktail lounge and liquor store. Every dollar we had went into the renovation. Jake even broke up his championship belt and sold the jewels. Later, people claimed he sold the stones to pay his attorneys in a criminal case, but that wasn't so.

Jake's lounge opened on our ninth wedding anniversary, November 9, 1955. It had air conditioning and special lighting, both of which were relatively advanced for that time. The bar stools and chairs were spotted leather. Three sports murals were on the walls with the most prominent depicting Jake flooring

Marcel Cerdan to win the middleweight championship. Outside, a large neon sign read, "Jake LaMotta's."

It was a nice lounge. Jake had everything going for him: a top location, good clientele, lots of publicity in the local press because of his celebrity status. It was the "in" place of the moment. All the entertainers who played Miami Beach came by for a drink when they were in town. Soon, photographs of Jake with some of America's best-known show business personalities were on the walls: Perry Como, Milton Berle, Kay Starr, Buddy Hackett, Martha Raye, Joe E. Lewis, and more.

Jake was excited. Both of us were optimistic. He was a good owner, supervising everything all the time. Then he started to drink with the customers. He got loud and obnoxious. People who were coming to meet the great Jake LaMotta didn't like him. The nice customers left. The wrong kind of people started hanging around. Jake's drinking grew worse—a quart of liquor a day. He began coming home at three and four in the morning, drunk, violent, and loud. He'd sit in our living room with the worst kind of people, his buddies from the bar. While the kids and I were trying to sleep, they'd get drunker, yell, argue, and laugh.

One night, he came home drunk with lipstick smeared all over his collar. I took his shirt, ripped it up, and threw it in the garbage. One thing Jake never did when we were married was raise his voice at me. His attacks could be violent, but were always quiet. Very calmly, he got up, walked to my closet, and took out the best dress I had, a pale-blue satin gown I'd made several years before. Then, still outwardly calm, he walked to the kitchen, lit the pilot light on the stove, and set the gown on fire . . . Back to the bedroom closet for another dress . . . And another . . . Once Jake started, there was no stopping him.

Very deliberately, he burned every dress in the closet; all because I'd ripped up one shirt with lipstick on it. Next, he pulled all my books off the top closet shelf and tore out the pages without saying a word. Finally, when everything in the closet had been destroyed, he looked at me and asked, "How do you like that?"

Things like that began to happen more and more often. Jake would come home drunk, wake me up, we'd argue, and he'd lose control. Then, as often as not, he'd start crying, "What am I doing? I don't want to hurt you. You're the only person I love." My reaction to it all was, this is very dangerous. I had to prevent the agitation, prevent anything that would make Jake angry. In the back of my mind though, I was starting to feel our marriage was over. The man I'd loved had become a man who mistreated and abused me. It was hard to believe I'd ever loved him. More and more, I'd look at him and tell myself, "If I met this man for the first time today, I wouldn't even talk to him."

But where could I go? In those days, a woman wasn't welcome in most places if she left her husband. And because of the way Jake had isolated me, I didn't have friends to talk with or confide in. I was all alone—I guess in a way like my mother had been—crying the way my mother had cried; silently, and never in front of the children.

Then, one night, I went out for dinner with a girlfriend at the Black Magic Room in Miami Beach. We walked into the restaurant, and there was Jake, at the bar with another woman. By then, I wasn't even jealous. I was beyond that; I'd had it. Jake looked up and saw me. I turned and walked out. He followed, caught up to me at the car, and slugged me, once, hard. The next thing I knew, I was on the ground, dazed, with blood flowing from my ear and a crowd of people gathered around me. Nobody did anything; they just stared. I got up in a daze. Jake very calmly drove me to the hospital, where a doctor put stitches in my ear. And I said to myself, that's it. I'm not going to take this anymore. I knew Jake was suffering. I felt pity for what he was going through. But I wasn't going to be his victim anymore. His problems were greater than my resources. I couldn't help him. I wasn't going to let my children and myself be dragged down and drowned by this tortured man.

In the summer of 1956, I left him. I hired a lawyer, got a legal separation, and moved out with the children. Jake kept the house. I could have fought for it—and probably should have—but all I wanted was to get away. I rented another place for myself and the kids. Jake was supposed to pay seventy-five dollars a week child support, but didn't. His approach was, if I needed money, if we were hungry enough, I'd go back to him. Meanwhile, I figured whatever it took was worth it. I'd have slept in the park before I went back to live with him. To make ends meet, I took a few modeling jobs. Then I sold my furs and jewelry. They didn't mean much to me. They were only possessions.

Jake took the separation as I'd expected he would: badly. He was constantly on the telephone, threatening, shouting. He sold the house and moved into a motel a block from where the children and I lived. Then he began coming over daily, like we were still a couple. Don't forget, we had three children, so the door to the house was always open with kids going in and out at all hours of the morning and afternoon. Jake would come by, sit down in the living room, and stare at the ceiling. Then, as often as not, he'd start questioning. "Where were you last night? Who were you with? When are you coming back to me?" I'd ask him to leave, or ignore him and keep doing whatever I was doing: cooking, cleaning, reading.

Then the real nightmare began. One night when I was home alone with the children, Jake walked in. He didn't say anything. Nothing seemed different from any of his other visits. Then he slugged me. And punched me again. In the past, he'd held something back when he hit me. This time, every punch was calculated to disable and cause pain, and the punches kept coming. Even now, it's hard for me to describe what happened. I still cry when I talk about it because I didn't think anyone was capable of hurting me that badly. There was nothing I could do. I was helpless and the punches kept raining down. Then fear set in. I stopped trying to protect myself. I couldn't feel the individual blows. I was paralyzed and numb. I realized that Jake might actually kill me. All I could think of was, who's going to take care of the children?

It was bad. When it was over, my nose was broken. Not one spot on my breasts was unbruised. There wasn't any white left; everything was black and blue. Jake left and I called a friend, Elaine Purpura. I needed her to take care of the children. Elaine came over, looked at me, and started crying. We were in my bedroom with the door shut. Then I heard a knock on the door. It was Jack, who was nine years old.

"What happened to my mother?"

"Mommy's okay," Elaine told him.

"I want to see her."

"It's alright, honey. I'm taking care of Mommy."

"Open the door. I want to see if my mother's alive."

That was the first beating. And there were more. Jake would come over and, if he wanted to beat me, there was no way to stop it. I got court orders; they didn't help. I went to the police; that didn't stop him. One night, Jake walked into the house. I could see what was coming because his face was red and he was hunched over like a crab, smoking. I backed away and, as he came toward me, I threw everything I could on the floor between us. A lamp, a cushion, chairs, any kind of obstacle, hoping he'd fall. Then I ran into the bathroom and locked the door, which wasn't enough because he began hurling his body against it. All I could do was wrap everything in the bathroom around me. I put a washcloth over my face and wrapped my head in a towel. Then I circled beach towels around my body. Just as I finished, the door frame shattered. Jake stormed in and started punching. I looked like a mummy, but thank God for the towels. When he finished, there were red blotches all over my body, but no real damage had been done.

Years later, I asked Jake about the beatings, and particularly the first one. "Why did you do it? What possible reason could you have had for hurting me so badly?" And Jake answered, "I did it because I loved you. I thought it would frighten you into coming back to me. Besides," he added, "I get hurt all the time. It doesn't mean anything."

It was bad. Whatever I did, Jake was on me constantly. He'd get drunk and come over to the house. I'd call the police and tell them, "I have a court order." The police knew what was happening, but somehow they never seemed to get there in time. One night, I found myself running down the street with a police car next to me and a cop leaning out the window asking, "Are you alright?"

Then I realized I'd run out of the house, dressed in my nightgown, to get away from Jake. Another time, I agreed to meet him at a restaurant to discuss our problems. There was another couple seated nearby. At one point, I said a few words to them. After the meal, we got in the car to go home and Jake started. "What were you talking to that woman for? Are you a lesbian or something?" I told him, "Jake, you're being silly."

Suddenly, without warning, he took his hands, dug his finger-nails—all ten of them—into my forehead, and raked them down my face. There were ten gashes bleeding.

As best I could, I sheltered the children from what was happening. They felt the tension; they had to know something was wrong. Still, I tried to maintain an atmosphere of normalcy. Maybe that was a mistake. I should have realized that sooner or later they'd be forced to face up to who their father was, but I wanted to protect them. The kids would get up each morning, eat breakfast, and go to school. In the after-noon, they'd visit the beach or play ball. They'd have dinner, watch television, do their homework, and go to bed. Finally, sometime around ten o'clock, Jake would come over and the action began.

And then, suddenly, everything changed.

Back in the 1950s, the police in Miami Beach were busi-nessmen first and law enforcement officials second. And what you were supposed to do when a cop came into your estab-lishment was treat him right; offer him a drink, give him a few dollars. Jake wouldn't do it. His attitude was, "I'm the champ; I don't pay anybody." More than once, he bragged to me, "No one tells the cops to shove it like I do." And he was right; no one did. Unfortunately, the cops didn't like him much as a result.

In January of 1957, a fourteen-year-old girl was arrested for prostitution. The police brought her to jail, questioned her, and learned that one of the places she'd been that night was Jake's lounge. The girl was living in incest with her father, who was a pimp. She'd been a prostitute for two years and looked ten years older than she actually was. Soon, the police devel-oped a theory that it was Jake who'd taught her how to dress, how to act, and what to say to prospective customers. Then they broadened their view to claim that Jake was operating a prostitution ring out of the lounge.

Jake was charged with maintaining and operating a place for purposes of prostitution, conspiracy, and contributing to the delinquency of a minor. On the day after his arrest, the *Miami Daily News* ran a front-page headline in big block letters that spanned six columns: "Nab LaMotta In Vice Case." Other newspapers followed suit. Jake was in trouble. So what happened? First, his mother came down to Florida and tried to patch things up between us. "Vikki, you and Jake belong together. You have such beautiful children. He needs you." She didn't understand. What could I tell her? "Mama LaMotta, your son beats me; he's a violent lunatic."

One concession I did make though, was to ask my lawyer to put a temporary hold on the divorce proceeding. Jake had enough problems. I didn't want the newspapers to report that I was divorcing him at the same time he was standing trial.

The trial itself took place in March. Jake admitted that some of the women who came into his lounge were prostitutes but denied any criminal wrongdoing. I don't know if he was guilty or not. Two of the charges against him were dismissed by the court. The prosecution agreed to drop two others. He was found guilty on the remaining charges, two counts of promoting prostitution, and sentenced to six months in prison.

One week before Christmas, after Jake's court appeals had been exhausted, I drove him to jail. In the car, he was philosophical. "It's funny," he told me. "With all the really bad things I've done in my life, I'm being punished for something I didn't do. Maybe life has a way of catching up with everyone."

The prison had eight cots in each cell, with a hole in the floor for a toilet. A guard let me accompany Jake as far as his cell, but no further. Jake let go of my hand and walked into his cage. At age thirty-five, he was back in jail, where he'd been twenty years earlier. It was a horrible moment. Here was a man who'd had everything—three children, the championship of the world, a wife who loved him—and he'd lost it all in an orgy of self-destruction.

For a while, I visited Jake every week in prison on visiting day. I even cooked for him: veal, eggplant, and his favorite pasta. Then a woman named Sally, who later became Jake's third wife, started visiting and bringing a friend, a stripper named Dixie. Dixie would walk in wearing a low-cut dress and tantalize the prisoners, who'd yell and scream. I thought it was ugly. I didn't want to be part of it. I figured if Jake enjoyed that, if he wanted Sally and Dixie, he could have them but not me.

Then, slowly, I began to feel free. For the first time in years, I wasn't afraid. Jake was in jail. He couldn't hurt me. One moment put everything in perspective. I was driving home from the supermarket with the kids on a weekday afternoon, when I passed a chain gang working on the highway. There was a guard with a gun and a dozen men with picks. One of the men was Jake. I brought the kids home, drove back to the worksite, and asked the guard if I could speak to my husband. He said yes, and I went over to Jake.

He was embarrassed to see me; happy, but embarrassed. He missed me, he said. The food in prison was awful. Then, slowly, Jake began to open up. His greatest fear was that the truck taking the chain gang to work each morning would be in an accident and overturn in deep water. The men would be trapped in chains, unable to get out, and drown. He didn't understand why he'd made the choices he'd made in life. "Vikki, I was a champion. I had everything and look at me now. You tell me; what happened?"

It was painful, for both of us. Jake had cheated himself. He hadn't enjoyed life. He'd inflicted as much torture and punishment on himself as he had on me, his ring opponents, and everyone else combined. But there was nothing more I could do to help him. I had three children to worry about and my own life to live. There was nothing good left between us. One month after Jake was released from prison, our divorce was finalized and I was gone.

Vikki is flanked by Jimmy Durante (right)
and Eddie Jackson.

Coming
of
Age

Chapter Nine

Being single was a new experience; strange, exciting, intimidating and, at times, overwhelming. Eleven years earlier, when Jake and I had gotten married, I was a child. Now I was an adult, on my own with three children to care for.

One of the first things I realized was how much I didn't know. When Jake and I were together, he'd signed all the checks and paid all the bills. If a repairman came to the house, Jake handled it. Whatever had to be done, he was in charge. After we separated, I had to learn everything on my own. How do you write a check? Who do you talk with at the bank to open an account? If a plumber or an electrician came to the house to fix something, I believed whatever they told me. I didn't understand the need for written estimates and a precise explanation of what had to be done.

Money was a problem. For a while, I survived on freelance modeling assignments. I wasn't with an agency. Instead, I'd read in the newspapers that so-and-so was putting on a fashion show, go in, and get a job. Then I worked my way onto the convention circuit at the Miami Beach hotels.

Different associations would come to town and hire me to sit in a booth and make popcorn or hand out pamphlets. To supplement my income, I sold most of my clothes. A friend of mine, Anita Tinsley, lived in the same apartment complex as a stripper named Bubbles Darlene. Whenever I needed money, I'd give Anita a dress, tell her how much I wanted for it, and she sold it to Bubbles.

Each day was a new day. Each day was a challenge. But the children were safe; we had enough money to get by; and I was happy. Then I got my first real job break, courtesy of Walter Winchell. We'd met at Jake's lounge several years before and he'd written in his syndicated column that I was "the prettiest girl in the United States." At the time, Walter had the power to control entertainers' lives; make them or break them. His column was that important. He was a man of strong opinions; good to his friends but his enemies were in trouble. I don't think he was ever married. I never saw him with an actual date and rumor had it that he was gay. But invariably, the women in his company were young and beautiful.

After I left Jake, Walter called me from time to time to ask, "How are you doing? Is everything okay?" Then he started inviting me out as part of his entourage when he came to Miami. Part of the deal was I could bring along anyone I wanted. He'd tell me, "All right, Vikki, we're going to this show and that restaurant. Get your girlfriends together. Bring one, two, as many as you want." He talked the same way he did on his radio program; authoritatively and fast. "Get ready, tonight we're going to have a lot of fun." And I always did; I loved being with him. Usually, I brought a girlfriend, so there were no social pressures. We'd sit down at the table, wherever we were, and Walter would say, "Okay, Rose, you sit here.

Susan, you're there. Vikki, you're next to me. Something's wrong; there aren't enough men for boy-girl-boy-girl."

One of Walter's eccentricities (if that's what to call it) was that he always carried a small pearl-handled gun. On occasion, he'd ask one of the women to hold it for him in her purse. One time, he loaned me money. I didn't want it. We were talking about something I needed for the kids, and he kept asking, "Why don't you buy it?" Finally, I told him, "Walter, I just don't have the money." He reached into his pocket, took out a wad of bills, and said, "Here, take this!" I didn't want to. I wasn't going to be anyone's charity case. "Vikki, I want you to take it. If it makes you feel better, you can pay me back." Finally, I took the money and, the first chance I got, I returned it. He wrote me a letter saying I was the only person who'd ever borrowed money from him and repaid it.

So that was Walter, in his sixties and going strong. I liked him a lot. Then one day, I saw an article in the newspaper saying that Jimmy Durante was auditioning dancers for a two-week engagement at the Eden Roc Hotel. Two shows a day, seven days a week, $125 a week. I hadn't danced professionally since the 181 Club when I was fifteen years old, but there was nothing to lose. I went to the Eden Roc, filled out an application form; and right away, I got scared. All the other women there for the audition were professionals. Then I heard someone calling my name.

"Vikki, what are you doing here?"

It was Walter. I told him, and he said, "You'll have no problem. Jimmy will love having you in his show."

I got the job, of course. That's how powerful Walter was. Then I went to my first rehearsal and it was frightening. Someone would tell us to do a particular step. I'd have no idea what it was, and the other dancers could do it. I'd thought the people running things would show us how. That way, I'd have a chance. Show me what to do, and I could do it. But these dancers already knew the chorus girl routines.

Not to worry. Midway through the rehearsal, the choreographer came over to me and said, "Vikki, for today, just watch and familiarize yourself with the routines. Jimmy wants you in the show. Don't worry about a thing. We'll help you learn."

So I took an envelope from my purse and wrote down the steps in a way I could understand as the dancers did them.

"2 steps, count of 6—strut 8—point back and forth—4 circle—6—up down—2—conga turn count of 4—plain conga—4 point steps—circle 6—mark time 16—8 point sideways...."

Thirty years later, I still have the envelope and memories of the job. Jimmy Durante was a sweetheart; a real doll. The way you saw him was the way he was. On opening night, he took me aside and said, "Don't be nervous; enjoy the show. Just go out on stage and have a good time. You'll be with me." He was absolutely wonderful and especially kind. Every night, he asked about the children. Once, he sent a huge basket of fruit to the house because he knew I was struggling. He wasn't a womanizer; he never flirted. He was a kind, sweet, soft, gentle man.

After the show's run ended, I went to New York for a week to visit my mother and father. By then, I'd let my hair grow dark again so people in Miami wouldn't recognize me as Jake's wife. My parents still lived in the neighborhood I'd grown up in and the feeling of deja vu was pretty strong. One afternoon, I was shopping in Manhattan when I passed a building with a sign outside that read "The Steve Allen

Show." I knew the show. It was on television every Sunday night, broadcast nationally. Each week, a different card girl would walk onstage to introduce the acts; one card girl for the whole show. I looked good that day. I was well-dressed and had a nice tan. On impulse, I said to myself, "National TV; why not try?" So I went inside.

There was a receptionist at the front desk. She stopped me with a polite, "Can I help you?" And I told her, "Yes, I'd like to be on *The Steve Allen Show*."

"Women don't just walk in off the street," she explained. "There are interviews and auditions. It's a long process."

Meanwhile, several men had come out to the reception area and thought the whole thing was pretty funny. They were laughing and teasing, and finally the receptionist said, "Wait here." Then she went into the producer's office, came out a minute later, and announced, "All right, the boss will see you."

The producer was quite nice. He looked me over from top to bottom, politely, and indicated they might be able to use me in a couple of weeks. But like the receptionist, he explained that there was a lengthy selection process. They had to do this; they had to do that.

"I'm going back to Miami on Tuesday," I told him. "If I do it, it has to be this Sunday."

Sunday was impossible. Someone else had already been booked for that night. I thanked him for his time, started to leave, and the producer said, "Wait a minute. We'll change the schedule and put you on Sunday."

That was how I made my debut on national television. The high point of my performance, such as it was, came when I introduced Lee Marvin. At the time, he was starring in a series called *M-Squad*. I was supposed to walk toward him as he came on stage. Then he'd grab my arm, spin me around, and

I'd ask, "Who are you?" He'd answer, "I'm Lee Marvin from *M-Squad*."

Except it didn't happen that way. Everything went as planned until Lee Marvin took my arm. Then he didn't spin me around like he was supposed to, so I just stood there. I didn't turn; I didn't ask, "Who are you?" He thought I'd spin on my own, and I was waiting for him to spin me because I didn't want to step on his lines. Everything seemed frozen in time. Steve Allen started laughing. Finally, Lee Marvin yanked my arm as hard as he could. I asked, "Who are you?" and the show went on.

The next morning, I got a telephone call from the producer. The first thing he said was, "We've gotten a hundred calls about you. William Morris wants to represent you." That was exciting. Those were the days when the William Morris Agency was top-of-the-line. I met with one of their representatives that afternoon, signed a contract, and soon I was commuting from Miami Beach to New York. I didn't have talent; I knew that. I wasn't an actress. My primary asset as a performer was my looks, but that got me by. Before long, I'd been on *The Phil Silvers Show*, *Gary Moore*, and *Steve Allen* for a second time. I began to feel good about myself and, for the first time since I'd left Jake, I began to think about dating.

Getting a divorce is a funny experience. Some people, especially men, think the minute a woman leaves her husband, she starts going out again. But that's not how it was for me. From the time I'd met Jake until I left him, I never had a date in any way, shape, or form. And after we separated, I wanted nothing to do with dating. Just give me peace, food on the table, and get me through each day without pain. Men were the last thing on my mind. That's the way it was for quite a while.

Then, one afternoon when I was in New York for a TV show, I was having lunch in a restaurant with my sister, Pat, and a man at the next table sent over drinks for the two of us. On our way out, we stopped at his table to thank him, and he asked, "Didn't I see you on *The Steve Allen Show*?" I told him yes, and he offered, "Why don't you visit my show?" I thought he was kidding. How corny can a line get? But he was serious. He'd just moved to New York from Nebraska and was hosting a TV game series called *Who Do You Trust*.

That in a nutshell is how I met Johnny Carson who, at the time, was virtually unknown. Pat and I went to the studio. After the show, Johnny took us for drinks with his sidekick, Ed McMahon (who laughed at all his jokes), and we had a good time. Then he asked if I'd have dinner with him at a jazz club later in the week and I said yes. For the first time in twelve years, I had a date.

The logical next question, I suppose, is "What's it like to go out with Johnny Carson?" Or to be more precise, "What was it like to go out with Johnny Carson before he became an American institution?"

For starters, I was a nervous wreck. I hadn't dated anyone in my life aside from Jake and, my first evening with Johnny, I felt like a teenager. I didn't know what to order in the restaurant. I was nervous about saying the wrong thing or eating too much. Still, he was good company and quite nice. His sense of humor was very much like it was in later years on *The Tonight Show*. He talked a little about his family (he was separated from his wife) and a lot about his clothes. He was straightforward, and I liked him.

Over the next few months, while I was commuting to New York, we had a half-dozen dates. Once, I remember, Johnny called me at my parents' (they had a telephone by then), and spoke with my mother. She was thrilled. "Vikki, he's such a nice man; so well-spoken and polite." From then on, whenever I saw him he'd ask, "How's Margie from the Bronx?" He sent me flowers and, on one occasion, perfume; Sortilege, his favorite. The problem was, I was afraid of a relationship. I'd had it with men. I didn't want to get involved with anybody. And after a while, I began to feel pressured, not so much by Johnny as by myself.

On our last date, he took me to dinner and, afterward, brought me to my friend's apartment in Manhattan where I was spending the night. It was late. He'd missed the last train to Westchester (where he was living), and asked if he could stay with us until they began to run again in the morning. My girlfriend had a studio apartment. Johnny and I spent the night sacked out on the floor with a pillow and blankets, watching movies on television. He kissed me a few times; but when you don't want it, you can let yourself be kissed and, at the same time, discourage more. That's what I did, and he was gentlemanly enough not to push it. He was attracted to me; I sensed that. But I was afraid. I didn't want to be involved with anyone, period.

The next day, I began asking myself, after sleeping together on the floor, what's next? Starting a real relationship meant eventually having sex, and I didn't want it. So I took the coward's way out. I left town without saying goodbye and, when I came back to New York, I didn't tell him. He called my mother quite a few times after that. "What happened to Vikki? When is she coming back? Please tell her to call me." I never did, and it was my mistake. He was a nice man. Maybe under different circumstances, something more serious would have developed between us.

Meanwhile, down in Miami Beach, even without dating,

I was getting on a pretty fast track. Again, my entrée was Walter Winchell. One night, he took me to see Frank Sinatra perform at the Fountainebleau and, afterward, invited me to a party in Sinatra's suite. There were quite a few people there. It was too crowded and, after a while, Sinatra got upset. "Who are all these people? What are they doing here?" He was working himself into a frenzy, pacing, stalking. Then he began singling people out. "You! Who are you with? Oh, really? Out! And you. Where's your coat? Inside? That's nice. Get it, and leave." One woman was wearing White Shoulders perfume, which Sinatra hated. He walked over, threw a towel in her face, and told her, "Go in the bathroom and take that slop off." She actually went into the bathroom and took a shower. That's how badly she wanted to stay at Frank's party. "No one invited you. Leave! I don't like your face. Get out!"

Gradually, the crowd thinned, and Sinatra came over to chat with me. I didn't know what to expect but he was polite. More than polite; charming. What struck me most were his eyes. They were his best feature, a very pretty blue; talkative eyes that betrayed a range of emotions. He was a fight fan and knew all about Jake, the good and the bad. At the end of the evening, he told me I was always welcome at his parties. For the rest of his Fountainebleau engagement, I went to the suite several times a week. I was attracted by the glitter; I admit that. And on stage, Frank was an exciting, wonderful performer. But behind the scenes, I didn't like what I saw.

Frank was a bully who thrived on insulting people and ordering them around. People took his abuse, partly out of fear and partly to bask in his glow. One night in his suite, a woman was snapping her fingers to a record that was playing in the background. Frank glared toward her and announced, "I hate people who snap their fingers out of rhythm." There was no reason to embarrass her like that, except he wanted to. And of course, she stopped. Another time, he had a fit because someone told a joke with a punchline that made him the butt. "You think that's funny? Get out and don't come back."

That was Sinatra. His sense of humor stopped short of himself. People kidded him at their own risk. Maybe he'd laugh; maybe he'd explode. Whenever something wasn't to his liking, he threw a tantrum, shouting, throwing things, turning over tables. He was impatient and often cruel, particularly to the people who served him. Invariably, the people he abused most were people who couldn't fight back.

As for our own relationship, Frank was constantly flirting, testing me. I doubt that he was romantically interested. Sexually, yes; romantically, no. There were times when I was in his suite and the group had dwindled to a few people. Frank and I would be talking and the others would start to leave. I'd say it was late, and he'd tell me, "No, stay a while longer. I need people around me until it's light out. I don't want to be alone."

I always left. I didn't want to put myself in that awkward situation where he made a move. Probably, there were a million women in the United States who fantasized about Frank Sinatra. But the truth is, I wasn't attracted to him. He didn't turn me on. And beyond that, Frank's reputation was that of a man who got around. "You slept with Sinatra? That's nice. How long was the line? You too? And you?" I didn't want to be in that category. And I didn't want Frank telling people that he had scored with Vikki LaMotta. I wasn't that way, so why should people think I was.

But Frank had a friend; a quiet, well-mannered man named Sam. And that changed everything.

Actually, I met Sam a day later than he and Frank had planned. One night, I'd been to a party in Sinatra's suite and left early to go home. I was in the corridor, waiting for an elevator, when Frank ran after me and asked, "Where are you going?" I told him I had to get up early the next morning, and he said, "Look, I want you to stay. There's a good friend of mine inside who's impressed with you and wants to be introduced."

I couldn't do it. Someone had to be up at seven to make breakfast for the children. Frank accepted that. He couldn't argue with taking care of the kids, but he made me promise to come back the next evening.

The following night, as usual, there were a lot of people in Sinatra's suite. As soon as I got there, Frank came over with his friend. The man was of medium height, lean, and balding. Not particularly good looking but with a presence about him. I thought he was a businessman. That's how he was dressed, in conservative clothes, wearing a thin gold watch. I figured he was about fifty years old, a year younger than my father.

Frank made the introductions. "Vikki, this is Sam, a very dear friend of mine. Sam, this is Vikki; she's a very classy lady." After that, Sam and I spent most of the evening talking. He seemed nice and asked a lot of questions about my children, which I liked. But what I couldn't believe was the way Frank catered to him the entire night. I'd never seen Frank cater to anybody. But now, the way people catered to Frank, that's what Frank was doing for this man. At one point during the evening, I mentioned that my daughter Chris, who was six years old, wanted a dog. Sam called Frank over and said, "Vikki's daughter wants a puppy. Let's get one for her." I mean, really! Someone telling Frank Sinatra to buy a dog! But the next day, I had a white toy poodle; and I was saying to myself, what a nice man.

After that, I kept going to Frank's parties and spent more and more time talking with Sam. Meanwhile, I began to see that, as deferential as people were to Frank, it was nothing compared with how they treated Sam. Finally, one night, I was in Sinatra's suite and things were getting pretty wild. Frank and Peter Lawford were throwing cherry bombs out the window. People were drinking more than usual. Then I heard a commotion in the hall. I went out to see what was happening and I freaked. One of Sinatra's flunkies was beating up a woman; really beating her, the way Jake had knocked me around. And all I could think was, get Sam. If anyone could stop this guy, it was Sam. I ran back to the room, brought Sam out to the corridor, and everything stopped. All he did was look once at the guy and the beating ended.

It was an emotional moment. The woman was badly bruised, crying and battered. Peter Lawford's suite was next door to Sinatra's. I brought her inside, made her lie down in one of the bedrooms, and put a cold compress on her forehead. Then I tried to comfort her. "It's okay; don't worry. Nobody will bother you. We won't let him in." And all the while, I was getting more upset because the beating had brought back bad memories and, looking at this woman, I was reexperiencing what had happened between Jake and me. At one point, Sam came into the bedroom to see if everything was all right. "I'll be in the living room," he told me. "If you need anything, holler."

I stayed with the woman until she fell asleep. Then I went out to be with Sam. We were alone and I started crying. Even though I didn't know the woman, seeing her beaten and bloody was horrifying. I felt for her, as though it had happened to me. Sam told me to lie down in the other bedroom, and I did. He asked if a glass of wine would make me feel better and, when I said no, he kept talking, quietly, gently. "That's the worst thing a man can do," he told me. "No one should ever hit a woman." And all the while, he was stroking my hair, touching my face, comforting me. I didn't feel he was trying to seduce me. If I had, I'd have been out of that bedroom in ten seconds. All he was doing was staying close, saying, "Don't worry; everything's going to be okay." I felt vulnerable, and Sam was there to protect me.

That's how it was. The evening went on and, as it did, Sam and I grew more intimate. It was a natural progression, easing the horror of what I'd just witnessed and the memories that had been stirred. Finally, almost inevitably as part of what was happening, we made love.

So there was a new man in my life; my first real relationship since Jake. And that meant I had special problems, because Sam was Sam Giancana. He'd learned his trade from Al Capone and Frank Nitti and was one of the most powerful Mafia godfathers in the United States.

Chapter Ten

After our first night together, Sam and I reverted to casual contact. One reason was that, although he owned a house in Florida, he lived primarily in Chicago. And more important, I wasn't sure I wanted to become involved with him. For a while, our meetings were limited to occasional dinners; sometimes with his friends, sometimes alone. Then one night, he called from Chicago and said, "I'm coming into town and I'd like to see you for the weekend. Meet me at the Fountainebleau. Bring the children, and I'll take you to my house in Lake Worth."

So we went to Lake Worth. I brought the kids, and they loved him. By Sunday night, they were calling him Uncle Sam. Then we started dating. I won't deny it. I was involved with Sam Giancana. By that time, I knew what he did for a living and I put it out of my mind. On occasion, I'd read something in the newspapers that forced me to ask, "Who is this man? What is he capable of?" But I'd grown up in a tough neighborhood surrounded by people who were connected with the mob. They were part of my childhood. And Sam never showed his ugly side to me. As far as the kids and I were concerned, he was a gentle man.

The house in Lake Worth was on the bay. Not extravagant, but nice; a typical upper-class Florida home. Most of the meals were prepared by a chef, who wore a big white hat and was treated like part of the family. Whenever I went to visit, the kids were welcome. Sam was a widower with three daughters, so he was used to children and treated mine as if they were his own. Chris was always on his lap. Once, he gave her a small barrel full of nickels, dimes, quarters, and silver dollars. But more important, he was sensitive to the children's feelings; even to the extent that, whenever the kids and I spent the night at Lake Worth, I slept in a bedroom with Chris, not with Sam.

Over time, our relationship grew more serious. I visited Sam in Chicago and met one of his daughters. We saw each other more and more often. The house in Chicago, which was where he spent most of his time, was filled with antiques: French provincial furniture, crystal chandeliers, paintings, urns, fine china. The best of his possessions were in the living room, which seemed like a museum the way he displayed his collection of German porcelain.

Upstairs, the rooms were fairly simple with a crucifix over each bed. Sam and I slept in separate rooms on the third floor when I was there. One of his daughters lived at home, and his aunt and uncle were there too. It was a family-type situation and he was formal about those things. From time to time, he held business meetings at the house. When those occurred, I was excused. Occasionally, we went out for dinner with underworld associates. But, when we did, business was never mentioned. The entire time we dated, I never discussed our relationship with friends. Silence was Sam's way of life. Without his ever telling me, I knew that to be so.

Looking back, I have a collage of memories about Sam. He

loved to cook. He was a lot like Jake's father in that regard. On a typical day when I visited Chicago, he'd make breakfast for everyone: eggs, toast, sausages, coffee. Then we'd go shopping and he'd stop at a bar or restaurant for a few "appointments." Lunch was usually eaten out at an Italian restaurant called The Armory. Afterward, we'd go home, and Sam would make telephone calls, receive visitors, or watch television. Often, we'd go back to The Armory for dinner; but on occasion, Sam would cook. "Vikki, you sit here. Have a glass of wine and eat some antipasto. No, you can't help; you're the guest." He'd do it all himself, including the dishes.

One of the days we shared that I remember best came just before Christmas when Sam and several "associates" asked me to go shopping with them to pick out presents for their wives, girlfriends, mothers, and daughters. Fur coats, jewelry, gold coins. You name it and they bought it; cash and carry. Sam loved every minute of it.

More than once, he offered me financial help, but I wouldn't take his money. It wasn't only that Sam was Mafia. I wouldn't take money from anyone. I was like my mother in that regard. One time though, he bought me a car. He'd flown into Miami and I was working that day, so I asked a friend to pick him up at the airport for me. On the way to Lake Worth, my car broke down and Sam complained, albeit disingenuously, that it would cost more to fix it than to buy a new one. That afternoon, he presented me with a brand new white-and-gold sedan. I can't say I wasn't happy. And he gave it to me in a way that made it hard to refuse.

A similar incident occurred during one of my trips to Chicago. Sam collected jewelry. He had drawers and drawers full of rings, watches, and loose stones. One of his prizes was a pure yellow diamond in a simple setting. It was huge. He asked me once, "Did you ever see anything like this before?" After we'd known each other a few months, Sam said he wanted to meet my friends and encouraged me to bring anyone I wanted with me to Chicago. One time I did, and Sam gave her a watch as a welcome present. Then he told me, "I just gave your friend a present. Now I want to give one to you too." He took out a tray with the most exquisite watches I'd ever seen. "Take any one you want."

I was embarrassed. I didn't know what the watches were worth. I didn't want to choose the most expensive. "Sam, I can't take a watch."

"You have to. I just gave your friend a present. She can't have one and you not." Then he reached into the tray and picked out a thin gold Italian-made watch with two amethysts, my birthstone, on the side.

And there are other memories; some fond, some less so. Once, Sam and I were going up an escalator at the Miami Airport when we ran into Rocky Graziano. Rocky grabbed me and gave me a big hug. Then, suddenly, he recognized Sam and turned white. He looked like he was going to die. "Sam, I didn't know. I'm sorry." He was scared. "Sam, forgive me. I didn't know Vikki was with you. Sam, it's okay. Vikki's just a friend." Sam didn't mind, but it was funny to see Rocky panic.

Another time, Sam took me to see "the old neighborhood" in Chicago. The house where he'd been born, the fish market, the bakery, the street corners he'd called home. It was a poor Italian neighborhood, a lot like the one I'd grown up in, and he'd traveled far. But always, there were reminders of the road chosen. Certain subjects couldn't be discussed. Certain places were off limits. Once, when a "business associate" got married in a Chicago suburb, Sam asked me to attend the wedding as his representative. "I can't go, Vikki. The FBI, the newspapers, they'll all be there with cameras."

I lived with it. I had misgivings but there were trade-offs. One afternoon, Sam telephoned me in Miami and said, "I'm coming into town tonight. Meet me at Frank's suite." I went to the Fountainebleau, and there was Sinatra, cooking in the kitchenette. No room service; no "let's go down to the hotel restaurant for dinner." Frank was actually making pasta.

Sam got there. Frank arranged the table very nicely. Everything looked wonderful. Then, to go with the pasta, Sinatra brought out a jar of pickled pigs feet. I thought he was joking. I mean, here's this jar with feet in it. They looked disgusting.

"How many would you like?" Frank asked me.

"None."

"Sam, how about you?"

"I think I'll pass."

Frank was incredulous. "But pickled pigs feet are a delicacy. I eat them all the time."

Not long after that, Sam and I were watching Sinatra perform on television. "Watch," Sam told me. "Frank's wearing a star-sapphire pinky ring that I gave him. He always holds it up as a signal to me during this song." And sure enough, Frank did.

I cared about Sam; I really did. But I wasn't in love with him. From my point of view, the relationship wasn't so much romantic as comforting. Sam was someone to turn to, a father figure of sorts. He didn't beat me. He didn't throw jealous tantrums. He made me feel appreciated and of value.

Then after we'd known each other for about a year, Sam told me that, when his youngest daughter graduated from high school, he wanted to marry me. I didn't feel that way about him. I didn't know what to say or do. If I stayed with Sam, my children would be financially secure. Regardless of what people said about him, when Sam and I were together, we were treated like royalty. Respected politicians would drop by our restaurant table to say hello. Maitre d's sent over complimentary bottles of their finest wine. Managers in the best hotels catered to him. I've always been treated nicely in public places, but people were in awe of Sam. He'd walk into a room, and everything would stop. That's how people responded to Sam.

Then something happened that brought me back to reality. An FBI agent came to my house in Miami Beach and began asking questions about Sam. That forced me to face up to who he was. I began asking myself, "How did Sam get to where he is? Does he really do these things?"

He did, of course. I just hadn't wanted to know. But one thing I did know; I didn't want FBI agents coming to my door. I began to think about what Sam did for a living and I didn't like it at all. I didn't want to be involved with a Mafia boss. And I didn't want my children associated with something that ugly.

From that day on, except for lunch once, I never saw Sam again. I didn't tell him why. There wasn't a confrontation. The next time he came to town, I said I was busy and couldn't see him. A week later, he invited me to Chicago and I told him I couldn't come because I had plans with the children. He didn't pursue it. After a few more calls, he knew. Still, Sam continued to keep in touch, telephoning periodically to say hello. And before long, I came to realize just how much about me he really knew. That story comes later on.

Meanwhile, my career as a "performer" continued to grow. William Morris was getting me jobs, mostly in Manhattan, and commuting didn't make sense anymore. Finally, in late

1958, I moved back to New York, rented an apartment in Yonkers, and settled in for what I thought would be the long haul.

Jake lived nearby. By then, he'd been released from prison, married Sally, and returned to New York. But of course, he didn't pay the required child support. One time, I went to court in an effort to enforce the financial provisions of our divorce judgment. Jake looked at the judge and said, "You think these payments ought to be made? You make them." Jake's lawyer turned white. Jake shrugged and added, "So what if they send me to jail. I've been there before." The judge ordered him to make the payments, and again I got nothing. Still, I tried not to speak ill of Jake in front of the children. And in a way I felt sorry for him. Nothing would ever fill the emptiness inside him.

So I was in New York, doing occasional television shows and modeling. Roberto Rosselini offered me a film role in Europe, but it meant being away for six weeks and I didn't want to leave the children for that long. I dated, but not often and nothing special evolved. To develop a relationship, you have to pursue it. Unless both partners work at it, nothing happens. I didn't have the time or energy for a man. My parents came over occasionally to help take care of the children. My sisters, Phyllis and Pat, were there if I needed them.

Then my father got sick. He was fifty-two years old and began having trouble breathing. Pains were shooting down his arm. He checked into a hospital and, instead of being put in intensive cardiac care, was given a regular room. A week later, he suffered a stroke. He couldn't talk. One side of his body was completely paralyzed. I went to the hospital every day to hold his hand and sit by his side. He looked like an animal in search of help, trapped, scared. We'd sit for hours and there was nothing I could do. I didn't want him to see me cry, so I tried hard not to. Occasionally, I touched his hair and brushed it back, but mostly we just held hands. The hand he could move was like a vice, a death grip.

Those final days, nothing could have stopped me from being with my father. Even if I had to clean him, open his robe to sponge him down, I wanted to be there. And he didn't want me to go. I could see it in his eyes. Then, one night, he went into a coma. He stayed that way for a few days and finally died. Afterward, my mother and I went to the nurses' station to pick up his belongings. In the pocket of his robe, the one he'd been wearing when he died, there was a photograph of me; a picture cut from a newspaper the previous year. In the photo, I was wearing a low-cut off-the-shoulder cotton dress, walking up a flight of airplane-ramp stairs. "He showed it to everyone," the nurse told me. "He really loved you."

The thing that struck me most about my father's funeral was how many people came. There were hundreds of mourners; not just from the neighborhood but from surrounding neighborhoods as well. He was a very well-liked man. The funeral home was packed with flowers. My mother showed very little emotion during the service. She didn't cry. She was quiet and very controlled as always.

After the burial, we went back to my parents' apartment. Most of our family and close friends gathered in the living room. I was in the bedroom with my sister Phyllis and her husband Tony, and Tony suggested we clean out my father's bureau drawers so my mother wouldn't have to do it. We opened one. It was full of playing cards. Decks and decks of brand new cards. The drawer was packed with them. We started laughing. I mean, how many decks of cards can one man own? Then my mother came to the door, quite embarrassed by the fact that we were laughing; at a wake, no less. She very sternly demanded, "What's going on here?" That made us laugh all the harder.

Once my father's affairs were settled, I went back to modeling and acting. In some ways, things were going well. I wasn't striving to be a star. All I wanted was to make a living, and that was happening. But even so, my days in New York were numbered. More and more, I found myself out all day, away from the children. Often, I had to work nights and didn't get home until the kids were sleeping. On weekends, I was too tired to enjoy the children and do active exciting things with them. I was making good money, more than I'd ever made in Miami, but spending more on rent, clothes, child care, and other expenses. So what good was it? The whole point of working was to take care of my children. What sense did it make if I couldn't be with them?

Finally, I decided I'd be better off in Florida, with fewer dollars and more time with the children. At least then, I could go to the beach when I wanted to and enjoy myself with a little less pressure. I knew I could get by in Florida. I'd done it before; I could do it again. So in late 1959, after a year in New York, I moved back to Miami.

Chapter Eleven

In Miami, once we were settled, I needed a job. Jack was twelve, Joey eleven, and Chris seven. I thought it was important for me to be home during the day so the children had someone to guide them. That meant working nights. Waitressing was out because the pay was lousy. Most modeling assignments ran between the hours of nine and five. Then I heard about an opening for a showgirl at The Latin Quarter. I went to the club, saw the manager, and got the job.

The hours were perfect—nine p.m. to midnight. Everyone in the show treated me well. I had some laughs and fun but, after a while, I felt uncomfortable. I said to myself, wait a minute, I'm a grown-up. I have three children; I'm thirty years old; and I'm on stage with girls ten years younger than I am. Also, from time to time, club patrons would recognize me as Jake's ex-wife. Jake had been a world champion and, somehow, it seemed out of place for me to be working where I was.

More important though, the job wasn't satisfying. It didn't challenge me. All it accomplished was feeding the children, and I was beginning to feel entitled to more than a cycle of struggle and survival.

Then one afternoon, I went to visit a friend, Barbara Klein. She was on the phone with someone in New York; a man named Tony Foster, whose father had just died. Midway through the conversation, she put me on the line to say hello. Tony was a singer with an engagement coming up in Miami. A few weeks later, when he came to town, he saw the show at The Latin Quarter and invited me out for dinner.

I liked Tony. He was talented with a beautiful baritone voice, polite, and very handsome with brown eyes, dark wavy hair, and even features. He was a year older than I was. The fact that we were both experiencing the loss of a father drew us closer. We went out together several times, and he was crazy about me. Very soon, he asked me to marry him. I didn't feel that way. I thought Tony was a good family man based on the way he treated his mother. He was always calling her, asking, "How are you? Is everything all right?" He liked my kids and seemed like a good person. But love? No way.

After his singing engagement in Miami ended, Tony went back to New York but besieged me with love letters, telephone calls, and flowers. Next, he actually moved to Miami to be closer to me and we became more intimate. Then I missed a period. "Oh, my God, I'm pregnant." But the next month, my period was back so figured "no problem."

Soon after, I heard from Sam. By then, he was in the midst of a much-publicized affair with Phyllis McGuire, who'd recorded the hit record *Sugartime*. Although I didn't know it, he was also involved in discussions with the CIA about mob involvement in a plot to assassinate Fidel Castro. Sam had kept in touch with me, calling periodically to say hello.

Mostly, we'd talked about the children. Once, the time we had lunch, Sam complained about the way Bobby Kennedy was directing the Justice Department. When Jack Kennedy was running for President, Sinatra had asked Sam to put his weight behind the Kennedy campaign. Sam hadn't wanted Kennedy in the White House, but acceded to Frank's pleas and channeled considerable labor union support to JFK. "And it was the biggest mistake I ever made," he told me. But in none of our conversations had Sam ever meddled in my private life. Our time as lovers had passed and he accepted that.

Then, one evening when I was visiting New York, he telephoned me at my mother's apartment. It was a shock, because he'd never called me there before. We had a few minutes of small talk and finally Sam said, "Vikki, I'm calling because I think you're doing something wrong. I understand you're seeing a man named Tony Foster; that he's moved to Miami, and maybe you'll marry him. I'm telling you as a friend, don't do it. He's not stable. He gambles. He won't take proper care of you and your family. I've made inquiries. I wouldn't be calling unless I knew."

Sam's warning led me to take a step back from Tony. I didn't resent his calling. He wasn't being possessive. He was looking out for me. Another month went by. Then, again, I missed my period. So now I was four months pregnant and didn't know what to do. It was too late for an abortion. This was 1962. Abortions were dangerous and illegal. For a while, I considered having the baby out of wedlock. But I decided that wouldn't be fair to the baby or to my other children. Tony was begging me to marry him. And finally, I gave in. I was tired of struggling, worn out from raising three children on my own. I was weak and vulnerable, more interested in security than love.

We were married by a justice of the peace. The only people at the ceremony were Tony, myself, and the judge. It was a cold, formal, one- two-three procedure. I did it for the children. I thought it was the right thing to do, and it wasn't. If I hadn't been pregnant, I never would have married Tony. Never. And even being pregnant, it was wrong. But there was one blessing. On July 22, 1962, our son Harrison was born.

On the positive side, once we were married, Tony tried to do right by the children. At times, he was too demanding and more critical of them than he should have been. But overall, he cared and gave them equal attention. It wasn't easy. Jack resented him from the start: "How can this man be my father? My father is Jake LaMotta, former middleweight champion of the world." But Tony did his best to cope with the situation. "You don't have to call me Dad," he told Jack. "You can call me Tony." But compared with the good, the negatives were overwhelming.

The first problem was, Tony was spoiled. He was used to being waited on and expected me to act like a second mother. I could be doing three things in the kitchen and Tony wouldn't lift a finger to help. He was constantly demanding, but make a demand on him and he threw a fit. Criticize him and he went wild. He was always telling me what to do to hold his love, all the things I needed to change about myself, everything he disliked in me that made him unhappy. But I didn't dislike those things in me. I wasn't unhappy with them, so they were Tony's problem, not mine. He wasn't a mean person. He didn't try to hurt anyone. But he was the sort of man who drains everyone around him until they've collapsed on the floor and he's still standing.

Worse, as Sam had warned, Tony was a gambler. I hadn't

seen that in him when we got married. But soon, it was apparent that whatever money he had he lost at the track. Several times, he hocked my jewelry, including the watch Sam gave me, to pay gambling debts. There was always money for clothes. He was a fastidious dresser and owned an incredible number of suits and sport jackets. But somehow, he was forever short when it came to living expenses. And he overdid everything. When he drank, it was too much. Once, he broke his leg falling down drunk. I'd tell him, "Tony, you can't drink like that." And the next day, he'd drive home from work soused, unable to walk straight. If he had a headache, he took eight aspirin. He'd get high on pills and talk and repeat, talk and repeat. Finally, I convinced him to check into a hospital treatment program for help. But right after his release, he reverted to pills and alcohol.

So there I was, with four children instead of three. Five if you count Tony. And I didn't love him. With Jake, I'd learned that loving someone and not having it work out is very painful. With Tony, I learned that living with someone you don't love at all is even harder to endure. I did things automatically, like a zombie.

Within two years, the gulf between us had widened to the point where we began sleeping in separate bedrooms. It was like having a boarder in the house, someone I wasn't married to; that's all. I would have gotten a divorce, but his mother was sick with diabetes and heart trouble, and we decided to wait until she was gone.

As a compromise, Tony began spending most of his time at the hotel where he worked as entertainment director. He ate at the hotel, slept at the hotel, left his clothes at the hotel. The house was a place to keep things in storage. We hardly ever saw each other. It was then that I started dating.

Tony knew it. He didn't care; he was dating too. But I wasn't comfortable with the situation. I don't believe in polygamous relationships. If I'm seeing someone, I'm monogamous. If the relationship goes sour, I won't cheat; I'll end it. I don't think I could enjoy having an affair with someone who wasn't my main man, my only man.

But there I was, technically married, dating, and it didn't feel right. I couldn't have someone pick me up or drop me off at the house. After an evening out, I couldn't invite a man inside. Suppose I met someone I liked? I was married with half a husband and four children; married and not married at the same time. Soon, I realized it made no sense to date. Nothing good could come of it. Then Tony's mother died, he moved into an apartment, and we were divorced. There's nothing more to say about our marriage other than I'm sorry for the unhappiness we caused each other. There are women who would have been right for Tony and vice versa. But we were very wrong for each other.

Once Tony and I separated, I was on my own again. As before, I worked as a model and dancer. In terms of money, the kids were fantastic. Jack, Joey, and Chris got parttime jobs and gave me a portion of their earnings. We made things work. We did it together. And you'd better believe, children appreciate the clothes on their back when they have to pay for them. Pants and shirts don't get crumpled up and thrown on the floor by teenagers who've worked for hours to buy their own wardrobe.

More than ever, I enjoyed being a mother. I began spending more time with the kids, going to concerts and ballgames with them. I loved watching the rites of adulthood unfold: Jack's first shave; Joey learning how to drive; Chris's first prom; Harrison having a crush on the girl next door.

But not everything was fun and games. Like all children, they had problems.

Jack was the oldest. From the time he was born, he was a quiet, serious boy. Growing up, he had a lot of friends but almost never smiled. At first, I thought it was just his nature. Some people smile, others don't. Then I realized he was unhappy because his father wasn't there. Jake was his idol, and Jack missed him.

As he matured, Jack clung to two things. First, a rigid work ethic. He had a paper route as a young boy and more demanding jobs later on. And second, he was a talented athlete with professional potential as a baseball player until a shoulder injury cut short his career. As it was, Jack worked his way through Miami-Dade County Community College and Florida State University. At Miami-Dade, he was the starting third baseman on the team that won the national junior-college championship.

Joey was more emotional than Jack; full of mischief, always jumping up and down. I suppose the handwriting was on the wall when he destroyed three cribs before he was a year old. Like the other kids, Joey was helpful around the house and athletically inclined; gifted at football and on the all-state wrestling team in high school. But one particularly sad event touched Joey's life. When he was eighteen, he got married. He was too young. I tried to stop it but he and his girlfriend Christy were determined to go ahead. They'd gone to high school together and, at that age, kids think they know everything. Then they had a child, Kim-Marie. Two years later, they broke up. Joey suffered a lot after that. He was terribly depressed and had constant headaches which the doctors said were psychological. After the divorce, Christy sent me a card that I still have. Inside, she wrote, "Dear Vikki, I just want to thank you for everything. You have truly been a great mother-in-law, but even a better friend. I hope we can continue to be close. Maybe we can take a trip together somewhere soon. Thanks again for everything and please keep in touch. Much love always, Christy."

Not long after that, Christy came to see me. She said she loved me and missed me, but had decided to remarry and didn't want to confuse her daughter by having too many grandparents around. She wanted Kim-Marie to think of her new husband as "daddy" and her new mother-in-law as "grandma". I couldn't believe what I was hearing. Kim-Marie was Joey's daughter, my only grandchild. I said, "Christy, let me just see her. I know you go to the beach. Let me come and play with her there. She doesn't even have to know who I am."

"That's not a good idea," Christy told me. Soon after, she and her new husband moved from Miami; I don't know where. Neither Joey or I saw Kim-Marie again. So Joey has a daughter, I have a grandchild, and neither of us has laid eyes on her since she was two years old. I doubt that Kim-Marie knows who we are. She's in her twenties now. I can't imagine a child not wanting to meet her family once she becomes a teenager. My guess is that she has no idea her grandfather is Jake LaMotta or that I'm her grandmother. If I could find her, I'd force the issue. I desperately want to see her and so does Joey. A child can never have too much love.

Anyway, that was the end of Joey's childhood. Chris, as the third child, travelled an equally rocky road. As a little girl, she was very sweet and tagged along everywhere with the boys. Of course, when it served her purposes, she'd rat on them to get them in trouble. She was ten when Harrison was born and was like a second mother to him. She cooked, she cleaned. There were times I felt I couldn't have brought him up without her. From age twelve on, she worked summers as a junior counselor. In high school, she had a part-time job during the school year as a switchboard operator at the Newport Hotel. But Chris was a child of the sixties. She got into drugs and went through a period in her teens when she was very self-destructive. Part of the problem—and we talked about it a lot later on—were her feelings toward me. As a teenager, she wanted me to be a typical mother. She didn't want me to go discoing with her. She didn't want her friends saying I was fun or great to be with. She wanted me to be fat, cook three meals a day, and stay home watching television like everyone else's mother.

Like Joey, Chris got married at age eighteen and the marriage didn't last. Then she had a particularly painful experience. Over the years, Jake had called from time to time, mostly to speak to me. Usually, I heard from him when he was upset; particularly after he divorced his third wife, Sally. Even when Tony and I were married, Jake would call the house and say, "Let me speak to Vikki." And Tony would complain, "He talks like you're still married."

After Chris left her husband, she wanted to find out who Jake really was, so she moved to New York and lived with him for several months. At the time, he was alone in a one-bedroom apartment in Manhattan, working as a bouncer at the Mardi Gras bar. Chris took a job as a barmaid at the Broadway Pub; a place that sold beer, hamburgers, and sandwiches. Soon Jake began to treat her like he'd treated me. If she came home ten minutes late, he'd call her a whore. If she was talking with a woman, he'd shout, "Get away from that lesbian." Every time Chris met a man, Jake would ask, "Did you go to bed with him?" After a while, Chris started to avoid him. She wouldn't come home nights until after Jake was asleep. She'd leave the apartment as early in the morning as possible. It was a place for her to crash, that's all.

Eventually, Chris grew into her twenties. She began to develop confidence and matured, realizing that she was attractive in her own right, physically and as a person. She told me once that, for a long time, whenever someone looked at her, she assumed it was because she had a rip in her pants or something like that. Then, finally, she understood that they might be admiring her for who she was.

So those were Jake's children. I'll have more to say about them later.

But for the moment, that leaves Harrison. He was the baby of the family and I spoiled him. Maybe I let him get away with more than I should have, and like his brothers and sister, he had his share of problems. For a while, he lacked direction and suffered from not having a strong father figure around. It took a while for him to get his studies in order, although eventually he did well in school and graduated from college. But I can honestly say that, as bad as the marriage to Tony was, one good thing did come of it. It brought me Harrison. He's a beautiful person, a blessing in my life, and I'm lucky he was born.

When Harrison grew into his teenage years, for the first time in my life, I had spare time on my hands. I started painting again, this time with oils and sold several portraits. I read a lot and made new friends. At last, I was able to put myself first and do things I'd wanted to do but never had time for before. When I was sixteen, I'd wanted to go dancing but married Jake instead. Now I could dance. When there were concerts in the Miami parks, I could go. I began to enjoy life more than ever; partly because I had time to enjoy it and partly because at last there was a foundation to build on. I had matured.

Then came the crucial question: "What should I do with the rest of my life?"

And then came *Raging Bull*.

Robert DeNiro as Jake LaMotta in *Raging Bull*.

Raging
Bull

Chapter Twelve

To a lot of women, turning forty is synonymous with disaster. Their looks have changed. Their children are grown. Against logic, they believe their best days are over.

I loved my forties. Physically and emotionally, I still felt young. No one was harassing me. I could do what I wanted. Then in autumn of 1976, I heard from Jake. His life was in shambles. The Internal Revenue Service was investigating him for income tax evasion. He and his fourth wife, a woman named Dimitri, had gotten divorced. His fifth marriage was on the rocks. Professionally, he was working in a topless bar to get by. So why the telephone call?

"Vikki, I gotta tell you something. Robert DeNiro wants to make a movie about my life."

Raging Bull, as the film about Jake was ultimately titled, had its origins in 1970. That was when Prentice-Hall published Jake's autobiography written with the assistance of Joseph Carter and Pete Savage. Pete was a man who'd do anything for money. He and Jake had committed several robberies together as adolescents. When I married Jake, Pete was in prison. After his release, he came to our house once for about thirty minutes. That was the extent of our social contact. Later, he got into the film business making porn films.

After Rocky Graziano's book, *Somebody Up There Likes Me,* was made into a movie, Pete convinced Jake that there was money in another fight-game autobiography. Jake supplied the raw data; Pete embellished it; Joseph Carter did most of the work; and in my humble opinion, the book stank. One thing that particularly upset me was the way Pete inserted himself throughout the story. This was a man who had hardly existed in our life. He was never at our home for dinner. We never socialized with him in public or at anyone else's house. The only time Jake even mentioned his name other than the one visit was when Pete was sent back to prison. Yet in the book, he made himself out to be Jake's best friend, like he was writing *The Pete Savage Story.*

Also, whole sections of the book were fictionalized. The wife named "Vikki" wasn't me. Some passages glorified Jake more than he deserved. Others made him out to be worse than he'd been. I mean, really! Jake was bad enough; they didn't have to make him worse.

The book got mediocre reviews and sold poorly. Then, in 1973, Robert DeNiro read it while filming *The Godfather, Part II.* DeNiro liked the idea of playing a fighter and sent a copy to director Martin Scorsese. Eventually, Chartoff-Winkler Productions put up development money for the project. Those were the main participants and they were good.

Like Jake, DeNiro had been born on Manhattan's lower east side. By the time *Raging Bull* was made and released, he'd starred in *Taxi Driver, Bang The Drum Slowly, The Deer Hunter,*

The Last Tycoon, New York, New York, Mean Streets, and *The Godfather, Part II.* Martin Scorsese, who Jake described as "a little guy with a beard who's a genius," grew up in "Little Italy" in the 1940s, so he also understood Jake's background and the random violence of urban America. Among his directing credits were *Mean Streets, New York, New York,* and *Taxi Driver* (all with DeNiro), and *Alice Doesn't Live Here Anymore.* Robert Chartoff (who went into the movie business after practicing law) and Irwin Winkler (whose show business career began as a mailboy at William Morris) were among the most successful production teams in Hollywood. Together, they'd produced twenty-one movies, including *Rocky* which was the biggest-grossing fight film of all time.

When Jake called to break the news, I wished him luck. We chatted for a while. At one point, I voiced the hope that the movie would be more honest than the book. That struck him as irrelevant. "Vikki," he said. "This movie is going to set me up for life. True, false; as long as I make money, I couldn't care less. They can make me a fag if they want."

That was the extent of our conversation. And since the movie was a long way from happening, I didn't think much about it. Then, a few months later, Pete Savage telephoned to report that one of the writers who was working on the screenplay for DeNiro and Scorsese wanted to speak with me. If they paid my way, would I come to New York? I said yes. Pete sent me airfare, met me at the airport, and brought me to an office in Manhattan. Jake was there with a third person, who was introduced to me as the writer. For several hours, I answered a barrage of questions and everything was taped. Then Pete went downstairs for a bottle of wine, the writer went to the men's room, and Jake just sat there with a sad look on his face. It bothered me; I didn't like the vibrations I was getting. So I said to him, "Look, Jake, I'm not sure I'm doing the right thing by being here. I don't trust Pete. Is this all right?" Jake sort of grunted, and I asked him again, "Jake, tell me the truth. I'm trusting you. Is this all right?"

"Yeah, don't worry. It's all right."

So I went back to Miami without any real sense of what was happening. But something still bothered me; the meeting hadn't seemed right. Another month passed. Jake kept in touch. And then things got serious. Pete sent me a screenplay in the mail. I read the script, and it was frightening. One scene showed Jake hypnotizing me, ordering me to have oral sex with Pete, and watching while we performed the act. Another segment—a dream sequence—had me in bed with a black fighter, one of Jake's opponents. It was trash. And I didn't know what to do because, if the film was made, millions of people would see me in that light. So I telephoned Jake and told him I was furious; that whatever had been wrong between us, it wasn't like that.

And Jake answered, "Vikki, I know it's not true, but Pete wants it that way. We need it to get the movie people interested."

If that was what interested movie people, then I wasn't interested.

"Vikki, if the movie people ask, you gotta play along and say it's true."

"No way."

That was that. I hung up. I wanted no part of Pete or Jake. Then a month later, Pete telephoned and said Robert DeNiro wanted to meet me. And as turned off as I was to the project, I couldn't say no to meeting DeNiro. Plus, if nothing else, this was my opportunity to be heard. Arrangements were made for DeNiro to come to Miami and stay overnight at my house. A new screenwriter, someone named Mardik Martin, was also scheduled to come, and I drove to the airport to meet them. In the baggage area, I recognized DeNiro immediately. He was dressed casually in a tan jacket and slacks. All I could think was, "Oh my God, Robert DeNiro." It was hard to believe that he'd come to Miami just to meet me. I introduced myself, and he told me to call him Bobby. Then Mardik Martin said hello. He was short with dark curly hair and a mustache. I liked him instinctively. We got in the car, drove back to my house, settled in the living room, and they began throwing questions at me.

"Why was Jake so jealous when you were married? Are you sure you didn't fool around? What about Pete? Was there anything between the two of you?"

And I got angry. The nerve of these people. Who did they think they were? But I realized that all they knew about me was what Pete had told them. They were seeing me through his eyes, and it was up to me to convince them otherwise. For most of the day, I tried to explain what it had been like to be married to Jake. How he was an unhappy man whose misery spilled over to everyone in his orbit. How ugly it had been; the fear and hate, but also the good things and the excitement. It must have been hard for Bobby and Mardik to understand what I was saying, particularly when I recalled something horrifying one moment and something nice the next. But as the day went on, they started to react differently toward me. I sensed they liked me and, more important, that they cared about the truth.

Mardik went to his hotel after dinner, and Bobby spent the rest of the evening questioning me about Jake. My son Harrison had some friends over. They were in the living room making a racket, so after a while we went into my bedroom to work. That's where I hung out most of the time anyway. The television was there. My girlfriends would come over, sit on the bed, eat pizza, and we'd watch TV or talk. Except it was different being there with DeNiro. I guess that's obvious. As soon as we got into the bedroom, Bobby stretched out on the bed with his hands folded beneath his head. I sat cross-legged; then eventually lay back, resting on an elbow. I liked Bobby. He was very low-key and easy to be with, genuine and nice. In some ways, he reminded me of Jake; all-consuming, driven less by motives than appetites. But unlike Jake, his emotions seemed balanced and in check.

So there we were, on opposite sides of a kingsize bed. Yeah, I thought about "it". And so did he; that was obvious from his body language. For most of the evening, one or the other of us had an arm dangling toward the center of the bed, inches short of the other's shoulder. There was a lot of laughing punctuated by pregnant pauses and touching on the arm to make a point. More than once, I told myself it would be the most natural thing in the world to make love. We were there alone. How could we not? Just for the wildness of it.

But at the same time, it didn't seem right. This was business. We were there for the movie. Bringing sex into the relationship could ruin it. Why complicate matters and do something that would lend credibility to the lie that I'd slept around and was unfaithful to Jake? Besides, I'd never made a pass at a man in my life. Whatever happened, it wasn't going to originate with me.

So we sat there; both of us aware of the sexual tension, both of us maintaining the separation between us. I could have done more to encourage Bobby's reaching out. Several times, I felt he was searching for a sign that he wouldn't be rebuffed. He couldn't have known it was all right. And maybe it wouldn't have been; certainly not later on for the future of the movie. That's what controlled it. I don't think either of us wanted to risk anything that would screw up the movie.

Finally, around two in the morning, Bobby asked, "Where should I sleep?"

"Where would you like to sleep?"

"Wherever you want me."

"You have a choice," I told him. "There's a bed here and a bed in the den."

"If I sleep here, where will you sleep?"

"I don't know. I guess I could sleep in the den."

There was a long pause. And I have to admit, by then I was telling myself, if he attacks me, that's cool.

"I'll sleep in the den," Bobby told me.

Later, after the movie had been released, several reporters asked him if we'd gone to bed together. "Nah," he answered. "Jake would have killed me." It was a good line, but I doubt very much that Bobby was afraid of Jake; not in the slightest. Rather, he was a professional who knew his boundaries and understood that bringing sex into business can ruin everything.

Bobby and Mardik Martin spent several days in Miami on their first visit. Most of that time, we talked about Jake or looked at scrapbooks and other memorabilia I'd saved from the marriage. Overall, I was impressed with the way they operated, but at times it seemed unduly repetitious. Again and again, Mardik would ask questions I'd answered earlier for the writer I'd met with Jake and Pete. For a while, I dutifully repeated my answers. Then I began prefacing each response with, "I already explained that to the other writer. Wouldn't it be easier for you to get the tape?" Invariably, Mardik would say no, he wanted me to answer again. That kept happening.

"Why can't you just listen to the tape? I don't want to go through that story another time."

Finally, on the last day, Mardik looked at me and said, "Vikki, I have to tell you something. You keep talking about the other writer. There was no other writer. There's nobody else. I don't know what you're talking about. I'm the only one."

That shook me up, and it wasn't until later that I learned what had happened. Apparently, Jake and Pete had a contract with Chartoff-Winkler Productions that entitled them to $78,000 each, but they couldn't get it until I signed a release. In addition, Pete wanted a certain type of screenplay to feed his ego. To accomplish those ends, he and Jake hired a phoney to masquerade as a writer for the production company. Then, the day after my trip to New York, they went to Chartoff-Winkler with what they claimed was my release and got their front money. I never knowingly signed a release. Either my signature was forged or else Pete got me to sign by saying he needed my signature on a voucher to be reimbursed for my airplane tickets. Thus, the phoney writer served two purposes. First, he got me to New York so Pete and Jake could claim they had my go-ahead for the movie. And second, Pete hoped the tapes from our interview session would bolster the credibility of the garbage screenplay he mailed to me later; a screenplay which I gather was never seriously considered by the movie people.

So there I was, with Mardik Martin telling me there had never been another writer. Jake and Pete had given Chartoff-Winkler a phoney release, which meant the movie people believed they could portray me on screen any way they wanted. And I was furious. My first reaction was to get on the telephone and blow the project out of the water. That's how mad I was. I wanted to kill everything. Then I told myself, wait a minute. More important than Jake and Pete getting away with the money was having a good movie. If the film portrayed me the way I was, if it portrayed our marriage the way it had been, if it was honest, that would be my payback. As long as the movie was true, I'd be happy.

Robert DeNiro was the perfect actor to play Jake. There was a wonderful writer and director. What I had to do was make them see the truth. It wouldn't be easy. Jake and Pete would do everything possible to color their perceptions. But millions of people would ultimately judge me based on what they saw on screen, and I wasn't going to let some actress pretending to be me blow Pete Savage on camera without a fight.

From that day on, I devoted an enormous amount of time and energy to the movie. Mardik Martin came down to Miami several more times and, at his request, I prepared taped recollections of my years with Jake. Once, after I mailed a particularly long tape, he telephoned to say how helpful it had been, and I felt like a child who'd just gotten a gold star from her teacher. Still, the battle with Jake and Pete raged on. And being involved with the movie carried the burden of being involved with Jake. Part of the price was being forced to relive a painful frightening period of my life. But just as bad, I had to deal with Jake in person all over again.

Over two decades had passed since we'd been together, and Jake still didn't understand the difference between right and wrong. He'd gotten older without getting wiser. He had no idea how hard I'd worked to raise the children after he'd gone. He seemed to think my life had been a lark for twenty years, that there'd been men around to pay for everything, and whatever men wouldn't pay for had come for free. As for

the lies he and Pete told the movie people, Jake's explanation
was simple: it was his wife's fault.

"Vikki, I do these things because Debbie's jealous. She's
upset on account of the wife they're showing in the movie
is you. I tried to explain to her, the picture stops fifteen years
ago; she can't be in it. But she won't listen. Every time she
hears your name, she goes crazy."

Then Jake and Debbie separated after a brawl at a private
social club in New York. According to Jake, there was an
argument, Debbie threw a drink in his face, and it shocked
him so much he threw his arms in the air and accidentally
hit her. Debbie's version was somewhat different. She claimed
Jake punched her, after which she threw a glass of water
and he knocked her unconscious. Regardless, she sued for
divorce. Jake counterclaimed, asking that he be awarded
alimony on grounds that Debbie earned $500 a week from
an illegal poker game in the marital residence. Ultimately,
Debbie won the last round by selling the story of their
marriage to a supermarket tabloid which featured the
romance under a headline that proclaimed, "Ring Champ
LaMotta's Wife Says Jake Made Her His Love Slave Under
Hypnosis."

So Jake was single again, broke, still violent, and drinking.
And he wanted me. At first, his attempts at reconciliation had
a poignant quality.

"Vikki, the greatest part of my life is happening now and
I want you there with me. I was finished, washed up, a bum,
gone completely. Then DeNiro comes along and everything's
different for me. I'm gonna be rich; people will respect me.
You and I, we had such a beautiful love story. You're the only
person I ever loved. The movie is fate. You belong with me."

I'd listen, and it was like a stranger talking. Jake and I had been together when I was a child. Now I was a woman in my forties. I couldn't make Jake happy and there was nothing he could do for me.

"You loved me once, Vikki. And I still love you. I've always loved you. I want to hold you in my arms and bring back my youth; kiss you and caress you. We don't even have to have sex together. I just want you to be with me. Please, Vikki."

There was no way, and I told Jake so. Meanwhile, Mardik kept working on the screenplay and I continued taping memories of life with Jake. At one point, I got a call from Pete saying Irwin Winkler wanted to meet me. I told him fine and made arrangements to meet Irwin at his hotel in Miami. Then I got paranoid, thinking it was another one of Pete's tricks. I'd never met Irwin and had no idea what he looked like. Finally, I telephoned his office, got him on the phone, and said, "Look, this is silly but I have to ask you something. Are you really coming to Miami to meet me?" Irwin told me yes. I met him and we drove around town to Jake's lounge, our old house, and other points of interest. A few days later, DeNiro called and said that he and a writer named Paul Schrader were going to the Caribbean to rewrite the screenplay. Pete was being taken out of the story completely and they were confident I'd be pleased with the end product.

It was about that time that I also had a final conversation with Mardik Martin. "You know something," he told me. "I'm a writer; my business is studying people. Even if I've never met someone, I have a pretty good idea of what they're like from listening to other people talk about them. But in your case, Vikki, I was one hundred percent wrong. Jake and Pete misrepresented you completely. I expected you to be a hard uncooperative, unpleasant woman, and you're not.

Good luck to you."

So Mardik was gone; Paul Schrader was in. And as much as I missed Mardik, I thought there'd be clear sailing ahead. But Pete wasn't ready to give up without a fight. Partly for revenge and partly to reestablish his role in the film project, he continued pressing to have me portrayed as a villainess. He was constantly feeding lies to the movie people and he still had a strong ally in Jake.

Jake was angry. Once his pleas for reconciliation had been rebuffed, he was obsessed by the thought of other men in my life. Soon, he was telephoning at all hours of the day and night.

"Vikki, this is Jake. Am I bothering you? . . . Okay, I thought maybe you had company, a man or something. I thought I heard a man's voice."

"That was Harrison," I'd tell him.

"Oh, all right. You know, I'm surprised I even got you on the phone. I mean, I figured you'd be out tonight. Are you sure that's Harrison?"

"Yes, Jake, I'm sure. Would you like to say hello to him?"

"Maybe later. You know, we're a lot alike, Vikki. I like staying home nights too. If I was down there, we could stay home together. You don't have a boyfriend now, do you? . . . I didn't think so. But you know, I hear things . . . Just things. Am I talking on the phone too long? I mean, maybe I should get off because some guy might be trying to call you."

Invariably, during the course of our conversations, Jake would ask if I was sleeping with X, Y or Z. One evening, Hugh O'Brien made the list. I don't know where that name came from. Maybe Jake had just watched a rerun of *Wyatt Earp* on television. After a while though, his primary obsession was DeNiro.

"Did you fuck him, Vikki? Pete says you did. It's all right; you're entitled. I just want to know. I mean, Bobby's the kind of guy who wants to get deep into his subject. I'm teaching him to fight like me and everything. So I figure, maybe to research the movie, he wants to fuck my wife."

After a while, it began to wear on me. I wasn't sure how much more I could take. I was getting it from Jake. I was getting it from Pete. All the bad memories of twenty years past were coming back to haunt me. At times, it seemed there'd never be an end. Finally, one night after a particularly abusive call from Jake, I sat down and dictated what I thought would be my last tape. I'd had some wine. I was down and depressed. My thoughts might have been a bit disjointed, but the message was clear. "Bobby, Mardik, whoever listens to this tape. I have to tell you something. To be put down by Jake, to still have all these ugly things and ugly people in my life; I got away from all that; I got away from that type of person. I don't have too many friends. I love to be alone. It took me so long to get over that ugly life with Jake. And now, the horrible gossip and bitterness; that kind of life, those people; I don't want any part of them anymore. The past few months, being a part of Jake again, listening to Pete, I don't associate with people like that anymore. Now I find myself involved with the same garbage. And I have to tell you the truth; it's not worth it. It really isn't. Let me be rid of Jake. Let me be away from that. I can't do it. If Jake doesn't want my name in the movie, please, don't have me in it. Make it Sally; make it Ida; make it Debbie. Please, everybody, just leave me alone."

Then I got angry. I'd worked too long; I'd tried too hard to make the movie people like me. There was no way I'd send that tape. I belonged in the film but I was sick of being asked,

"Why was Jake so jealous? Why would he tell us awful things that weren't true? Are you sure you never slept with Sugar Ray Robinson? What about Jake's brother Joey?"

One way or the other, I figured I'd end it. So I sat down and dictated a second tape. And this one I sent.

"For quite a while, you people have shown an uncommon curiosity in who I've slept with. Therefore, you should know the following. While Jake and I were married, I slept with Rocky Graziano, Rocky Marciano, Rocky Castellani, Edward G. Robinson, each of Jake's brothers, every active member of the New York Yankees, and the entire eighth division of the United States Marine Corps. After we were divorced, I slept with Sugar Ray Robinson, Sugar Ray Leonard, Sugar Ray Seales, Mickey Mantle, each of Jake's wives, and the entire roster of several National Football League teams. Now that you have this information, I trust the subject will not be mentioned between us again."

And it wasn't.

Chapter Thirteen

Raging Bull marked a turning point in my life. It was the first time I fought to make something important happen, took control, and won. Pete died of a heart attack soon after the movie was released, and since then I've tried to give him his due. He worked hard to sell the project; he hustled it well. But there was no excuse for the way he tried to exploit me and use the film to his own advantage at my cost. That part of his character served no one well and we were at odds till the end.

Meanwhile, as work on the screenplay progressed, DeNiro and I maintained contact. One incident between us was rather awkward. I was in New York and Bobby took me to lunch. I don't have the greatest wardrobe in the world, mostly sandals, T-shirts, and jeans. They're comfortable and inexpensive. Midway through the meal, I realized Bobby was staring at my sandals. They were white with high heels; nothing out of the ordinary, except one of the straps had broken just before I left for New York and I'd pieced it together with scotch tape. What could I say? I'm trying to make my shoes last longer? Don't look at the scotch tape?

My foot felt paralyzed, like a rattlesnake was coiled nearby, ready to strike if I moved an inch.

It was during the same lunch that Bobby told me a little about his philosophy of acting. In order to play a character, he has to empathize with that person. At the time, I thought I understood what he was saying. Later though, I realized I hadn't grasped the scope of it at all. Bobby did more than empathize with Jake. He began to act like him, talk like him, even think like him. One afternoon, I went to watch them work out together at Gramercy Gym. The screenplay required Bobby to be in the ring. For about a year, he had trained with Jake, learning fundamentals and sparring hundreds of rounds. Standing by the ring apron, watching them spar, was as strange a feeling as I'd ever known. Jake had trained Bobby to fight the way he'd fought as a young man. Right in front of my eyes, Jake number one and Jake number two were fighting each other.

Around the same time, Chris invited Bobby and me to her apartment for dinner. He hardly said anything the entire night. Mostly, he sat on the sofa and watched us talk. Chris kept saying, "You're in my house, relax; take your shoes off; put your feet on the coffee table." Bobby wouldn't let up. The whole time, he was very intense until, as the evening wore on, I realized he was imagining himself as Jake, spending time with his wife and daughter. That's who he'd become and I began to think of him in those terms.

One night, the telephone rang. I picked up the receiver, and right away I knew it was Jake because I heard low guttural sounds. Jake ruined his nose when he was fighting. As a result, he has trouble breathing. Before he speaks, either he takes a deep breath or tries to drag air in through his nose. Whenever he calls, before he says a word, I know it's him.

So I said, "Jake?" And a voice answered, "No, it's Bobby." It was incredible. He'd mastered Jake's mannerisms to the point where, without even speaking, he sounded like him on the telephone.

Finally, just before filming began, I met Martin Scorsese for the first time. Chartoff-Winkler flew me to New York. Then Bobby and Marty came to see me. I liked Scorsese. Bobby had told me I would, and I did. He's a small hyper man, very intelligent and quick to judge. In many ways, he and DeNiro are opposites. Bobby moves and speaks slowly. Marty does everything as fast as possible. But they're remarkably alike in their view of the world and seem to communicate with each other without even talking.

At our meeting, we chatted a bit. Then Marty told me, "Vikki, the screenplay is finished. What we'd like now is to read it to you. Bobby will play Jake. I'll read all the other roles. Anytime something strikes you as wrong, whether it's a major inaccuracy, a minor change, something you don't like, I want you to interrupt us."

What a trip! They started reading, and I had a ball. Every now and then, Bobby would stop and ask, "How do you like that?" I'd answer "great" or "okay" or "maybe you should change it." Overall, I was happy with what they read me. It was true to Jake's life and our marriage. But I was painfully aware that changes might be made. There was no guarantee that I'd be happy with the end result.

Filming began in April 1979. Thereafter, Scorsese or someone else would call periodically for information. "We're on the set, shooting this scene, and don't know what Jake would have done. How would he have reacted? What would you have said in return?" Then one afternoon, Jake telephoned and told me, "I'm in California watching them do fight scenes for the movie. Marty says, if you want to come, they'll pay your way."

I wasn't sure Marty really wanted me there. More likely, Jake had pressed for the invitation but it sounded like a unique experience. How could I not go? So I flew to California, checked into the hotel and, the next day, went to the stadium where the fight scenes were being filmed. The arena was jammed with people dressed in costumes from the 1940s. Jake and I sat together, watching it all. Bobby looked great. By then, he was proficient enough as a fighter to have cracked one of Joe Pesci's ribs during filming. He and Scorsese working together were like two critical masses coming together in a brilliant fiery ball.

After a while, they took a break. Bobby and Marty stayed by the ring. Jake was excited by the way it looked from the stands and took my hand. "Come on. I want to tell them how great it was." I said okay and we walked through the crowd to the edge of the ring. Marty was sitting on one of those director's chairs that rises up in the air with a boom and camera. He was at ring level, just inside the ropes talking with Bobby. He saw us coming; they both did. And they ignored us. Jake walked to within five yards of them, to the edge of the ring. All he wanted was for one of them to turn around and acknowledge his presence. They wouldn't do it. I said, "Jake, let's go." And he told me, "No, I just want to tell them. I want them to know how good it looked."

For ten minutes, we stood there. It seemed like an eternity. I was embarrassed for Jake. He was caught and didn't know how to walk away from them. Finally, he started calling, "Marty, Marty. Over here."

Scorsese turned and Jake told him, "It's beautiful." That's all he wanted to say. Marty answered, "Thank you," and turned back to DeNiro.

Soon, I got a taste of the same medicine. Filming moved to New York, and my sister Pat telephoned to say that one of her friends lived directly behind the Bronx shooting location. "It's unbelievable," she told me. "The house looks just like the one you and Jake lived in. Robert DeNiro is in the backyard now with three children. The woman who plays you has a turban on her head. Vikki, she's beautiful."

How could I stay away from something like that? Later in the week, I flew to New York. Pat took me to her friend's house, where we sat in the backyard and watched them film. Then we went over to the set to say hello. And as soon as we got there, I knew it was wrong. Scorsese didn't want to see me. It was written all over his face, as though he was holding a placard that read, "Vikki, go home." I started to leave. Then a tall blonde woman saw me and said, "Vikki, wait a minute. I want to meet you."

It was Cathy Moriarty, the woman cast to play me in the movie. She was nineteen years old, a receptionist without any acting experience at all. We'd never met. I'd had no idea what she looked like. And there she was. We talked for a bit. I liked her. Then Marty called over to say it was time to resume filming. I left and didn't go back again.

From then on, my contacts with the movie people were minimal. I'd done my job; they were doing theirs; and everybody seemed satisfied. Late in the year, they sent me a check for $25,000 in exchange for a release and the time I'd devoted to the project. Then filming stopped while Bobby, who normally weighed 150 pounds, gained sixty pounds to portray Jake at age forty. He could have used make-up but that's not the way DeNiro operates. He wanted to feel what a fat person feels, experience the bloat. During the weight-gaining process, his health was monitored by a doctor, who wasn't particularly pleased with what was happening. Bobby's blood pressure rose. The insides of his thighs developed rashes from rubbing together. His feet hurt from the added weight. He was constantly huffing and puffing. His own daughter was embarrassed to be seen with him.

Finally, the film was edited. In September 1980, publicity began with full-page newspaper ads across the country. That's when I started to get frightened. All of a sudden, I realized that there was no stopping the movie; that an entire nation would see me portrayed on screen; and I didn't know what that portrayal would be like because I still hadn't been allowed to see the film. Jake was in the same boat. He hadn't seen it either. Several weeks before the premiere, he told me that he'd been to the movies and seen a coming attraction for *Raging Bull*. "Vikki, I was so nervous I almost left the theater. I couldn't see what I was seeing." Both of us knew our lives were about to change but neither of us knew how. It was an odd bond. In a strange way, we'd been reunited.

The world premiere was in New York on November 14, 1980. Chartoff-Winkler flew me up from Miami so I could attend with Jake. Jack, Joey, Chris, and Harrison were also invited. That morning, I gathered the family together and gave everyone a little speech. "Look," I admitted. "I don't know how I'm going to react to this. I might like the movie. I might hate it. Maybe I'll sit there crying and carrying on like a lunatic or leave because it's too painful to watch. I just don't know."

That afternoon, I went to the theater to check out the seats. I wanted to be in back, near an exit, so if I did leave, it wouldn't be noticed. Then I went to a men's clothing store and bought six handkerchiefs, just in case.

That night, Jake looked very handsome. He wore a white shirt, conservative tie, and elegant grey suit. We met at the hotel and walked to the theater. All six of us; Jake, the four children, and myself. Except they weren't children anymore. They were adults. Outside the theater, there were dozens of photographers with flashbulbs popping. I saw Cathy Moriarty. She was with her family. I don't think DeNiro was at the showing. Generally, he avoids interviews and public appearances. Jake loved the attention. He kept saying, "Look at this, I'm a star." He was all smiles.

We took our seats, the ones I'd chosen in back near an aisle. The lights dimmed. The movie began. And all of a sudden, on the screen, there was a man, DeNiro, wearing a hooded robe, dancing in slow motion framed by three ring strands against a backdrop that vanished into mist. Low music was playing. And I said to myself, "Oh my God, this is incredible." I don't know how else to describe it. Anyone who's seen the movie knows what I mean. There was a spiritual quality to what was happening. It was extraordinary.

Martin Scorsese hadn't made a movie about boxing. It was about Jake—his mind and character; the violence, paranoia, ugliness, and rage that scarred his life. Part of the film involved fight scenes; the most graphic violence I'd ever witnessed on screen. I hid my eyes during those moments. Other segments were soft with Italian arias playing.

There were several things I didn't like. At times, the film was a bit disjointed. In a couple of scenes, it portrayed me through Jake's eyes rather than the way I was. And I wish they'd shown more of the good in our marriage instead of just the bad. But basically, *Raging Bull* captured what Jake and I were about. It's essence was truth. Robert DeNiro was Jake. I laughed; I cried; I loved every moment. And I told myself, thank God for what I did. Thank God I fought to make Bobby, Marty, Mardik, and all the others see me the way I am instead of the way Pete portrayed me.

When the movie ended, the audience seemed stunned. That's how overwhelming DeNiro's performance had been. People weren't sure whether to applaud or weep. Jake was sitting directly beside me.

For a long time, he was silent.

"Jake, did you like it?"

"I don't know," he said finally. "I could see this movie ten times and not know what to think." His face had a confused, bewildered look. "DeNiro is great. He's really me. But I see that man on screen. I know I've done all those things, and I don't like that person. He's a bad man, and I know it's me."

That was what Jake said to me. And then I realized he'd given everything he had to the movie. He'd spilled his guts, opened up completely, expecting a film like *Champ* or *Rocky* that would restore his dignity. Never in his wildest dreams had he expected to be confronted so starkly by the dark side of who he was. And I told myself, sure, I can sit back and enjoy the movie. The way I'm portrayed is fine. It's easy for me. But suppose everything in my life that I'm ashamed of had been thrown in my face. Imagine if all my negatives were on screen for millions of people to see. That's what had just happened to Jake, and he was ashamed.

After the premiere, I saw the movie a dozen times. Alone, with friends, with family, in varying environments. I wanted to get as many different feelings and sensations as possible. I even saw it twice more with Jake. Then as the days passed, I started to feel a bit overwhelmed by the attention I got. Having been married to a world boxing champion, I was used to the limelight. But *Raging Bull* was a major movie with a towering performance by DeNiro. Whether critics liked it or hated it, they wrote about it, and that brought my name to millions of people who'd never heard of me or Jake. Also, Chartoff-Winkler had hired me to go on a national publicity tour; and when that began, the exposure I received increased exponentially.

Jake was erratic during the promotional period. Sometimes he'd be kind and gentle. On other occasions, he was awful. I think what was going on was, he realized he still loved me. We were together daily. He was starting to feel that rightfully I belonged to him. But he knew I was gone and it made him miserable. Over and over, he'd tell me, "Vikki, I love you. Please marry me. We don't even have to have sex. I just want you to be my wife and live with me."

I'd tell him no. Then, as often as not, the conversation would turn ugly. "You don't understand, Vikki. Right now, you're nothing. You're a nobody. You need a man to pay the bills and you have to fuck for it. That's what I want. You've had sex with slobs before. You could fuck me."

"Jake, stop it."

"Please, Vikki. I'm tired of this shit. I want to be happy. Don't you need love and affection? Aren't you curious after all these years? Let's you and me go to bed together. Make me happy."

"Jake, make me happy. Leave me alone."

"Go fuck yourself."

That's how it was with Jake. He was a sad caricature of himself, reaching out for someone who wasn't there anymore.

The publicity tour lasted a month and was followed by a second six-week tour in Europe. Flying over the Atlantic Ocean, Cathy Moriarty and I were the only people in first class. It was a nighttime flight and we had a first-class dinner: caviar, lobster, chateaubriand, and champagne served on white linen with candles. Midway through the flight, a stewardess came over and said the pilot wanted to meet us. We went up to the cockpit, looked out the window, and the stars seemed on top of us. Millions and millions and millions of stars on black velvet. It was a beautiful night.

I'd never been to Europe before, and Cathy was a good traveling companion. We had a lot in common, both of us coming from large Bronx working-class families. The only country I wanted to see that we didn't visit was Italy. Otherwise, it was a dream trip. Everywhere we went, I was captivated by sights, sounds, and people. The tour was scheduled so Jake was in France the same week we were. One night, we went to the Follies Bergere together, Cathy, Jake, and myself. But the only thing that seemed to interest Jake was a trained dog act. Showgirls paraded around semi-nude for an hour and he was half-asleep. Then two little dogs came on stage. Jake sat up straight and blurted out, "Look at that!"

After the tour, we sat back and waited for the Academy Awards. *Raging Bull* had received eight nominations. Best picture, actor, director, cinematography, film editing, achievement in sound, and supporting actor and actress. I was hoping desperately that Cathy would win. I also wanted to be there for the ceremony rather than watch it on television, but I wasn't invited.

Several days before the ceremony, Jake telephoned and asked when I was going out to Hollywood. I told him the truth; that Chartoff-Winkler hadn't given me a ticket. Then Jake did something nice. He called DeNiro. Bobby spoke to the powers that be, and a day later everything was set. "Here's your airplane ticket. Here's your ticket for the awards ceremony. When you get to the coast, there will be a room in your name at the Beverly Wilshire."

That was great. I flew to Los Angeles the day before the awards, went to the hotel—and there was no room for me. Cathy Moriarty and I had spoken a week earlier, and she'd told me, "If you come and don't have a room, you can share with me." I tried getting in touch with Cathy, but she'd gone out with her boyfriend and left word at the front desk that she wouldn't be back until morning. The hotel was sold out.

Enter Jake. He and Jack were sharing a room at the Beverly Wilshire. "Come on, Vikki. You can sleep with me."

"I'm not sleeping with you, Jake."

"I don't mean that way. Jack and I have twin beds. I'll take one, you take the other, and Jack can sleep on the floor. He's your son. You can trust him for the night even if you don't trust me."

So twenty-five years after I'd left Jake, we spent the night together at the Beverly Wilshire with Jack on the floor between us. The next day, a room at the hotel opened up— I think DeNiro handled that too—and things settled down a bit.

The awards ceremony was vintage Hollywood. Johnny Carson was master of ceremonies, another reminder of my life a quarter-century earlier. Cathy Moriarty lost out to Mary Steenbergen for best supporting actress. *Ordinary People* won the Oscar for best picture. The nominees for best actor, in addition to DeNiro, were Jack Lemmon, Robert Duvall, John Hurt, and Peter O'Toole.

Bobby won.

Afterward, Jake and I went to the Board of Governors Ball at the Beverly Wilshire Hotel. We stayed for a while to see what it was like; then spent the rest of the night at a private party DeNiro gave at a small Italian restaurant. Maybe fifty of us were at the dinner. Most of the evening, I went around saying goodbye to people I'd never see again. They'd been part of my life for four years, but now the movie was done and I knew they'd be gone.

So that was it. *Raging Bull* was over. Looking back, I'm pleased with it all. The movie people I met were straight and honest with me. Sometimes they overlooked things that would have made me feel better, like the way they handled the Academy Awards. But only two things they did really bothered me. One of them is silly—they spelt my name wrong. In the film credits, in advertising, everywhere, they wrote "Vickie" instead of "Vikki." I'd sent them loads of letters. They'd seen my name in print dozens of times. I'd assumed they were observant enough to get it right, and I was wrong.

The other oversight hurt more. During the research stage of the project, I'd loaned the movie people whatever they wanted. Photo albums, scrapbooks, family films, all sorts of personal memorabilia. A lot of that material was never returned. Home movies that were very special to me got lost in the shuffle. Someone stole a series of photo folders I'd saved from the Latin Quarter and Copacabana. Someone else—I think it was Jake's wife—took the scrapbook I'd maintained during his career and destroyed every picture of me. Bobby and Marty seemed genuinely concerned when I told them about the lost items. I don't think it was their fault, but some of the people working for them weren't as conscientious.

After the Academy Awards were over, I returned to Miami. For a while, it was nice just to relax and be at home. But then I started to feel let down. Harrison was eighteen and on his own. Everything I'd undertaken up until then was done. My life was quiet; I was living alone. I began to ask, what happens now?

Then *Playboy* came along.

Vikki at age fifty-one.

Playboy

Chapter Fourteen

Society promotes the idea that twenty-year-old women are more sexually desirable than women of forty. Women of fifty are considered over-the-hill, ready to be put out to pasture.

At age fifty-one, I posed nude for *Playboy*. Sometimes I tell people the only pictures I thought I'd be taking at that age were X-rays, not X-rated. But there's a serious side to the story.

Posing for *Playboy* had its origins in an article Joe Flaherty wrote about *Raging Bull* for *Inside Sports*. A photographer named Ken Regan was hired by the magazine to take pictures of Jake and myself, and during the session he said I was photogenic.

"Yeah," Jake added. "She'd be perfect for *Playboy*."

We laughed, all three of us. Coming from Jake, it was ridiculous. Here's this crazy jealous man, suggesting I do *Playboy*. After the session ended, Ken walked me to the elevator and asked if Jake meant it. "Probably," I answered. The next day, I flew back to Miami and forgot about it. *Raging Bull* had just been released, and I was getting ready to go on tour. Then, a week later, Ken telephoned and said he'd talked with *Playboy*. "Vikki, they're very interested. Could you send me a photo of yourself in a bathing suit?"

I didn't take him seriously. Why would *Playboy* run a picture of a fifty-one-year-old woman in a bathing suit? It was silly but I was flattered, so I mailed him several snapshots of me in a bikini. They were ordinary photos that Chris had taken a few months earlier. Then Ken called again to say that *Playboy* had seen the photos and was considering a layout— "the usual glamour photography." I asked what that meant, and he told me "nude shots."

That wasn't what I'd had in mind. Not at all. My answer was no. End of story (I thought). Cathy Moriarty and I went off to Europe to publicize the movie. Then I managed my way to Hollywood for the Academy Awards and, the night after the ceremony, had dinner with Jake at the Beverly Wilshire.

The restaurant was crowded. Jake and I had reservations. When we got there, the maitre d' led us past two men who were sitting together. I'm used to people looking at me, but this was different. Both men stared as we went by. It was very noticeable, not at all subtle. They simply stopped eating and followed me with their eyes until we were seated. The waiter brought menus. Jake and I ordered. Then one of the men came over and said, "Vikki, I just want to introduce myself. I'm Gary Cole, the photography editor for *Playboy*. We're very disappointed you didn't do a layout with us."

That was Jake's cue. Right away, he started. "Yeah, she should do it. Wouldn't she be perfect?" I told him, "Jake, you're being silly." But he kept at it. "No, it would be fantastic. Really, Vikki, you'd be great."

Anyway, Gary Cole went back to his table. Jake finally

changed the subject and we ate dinner. Afterward, it was only ten o'clock. Jake took the elevator upstairs and went to bed. I had my own room by then, and decided to visit some of the movie people who were in the cocktail lounge. I walked in, and there was Gary with his dinner companion. I stopped by their table. We chatted. They bought me a drink. And Gary said, "I wish you'd reconsider. The pay is good. But more important, you're a beautiful woman. We have glamour photographers who would do the job right. Try to be open-minded about it."

We talked for an hour. I was intrigued, but hardly convinced. Then, the next morning, Gary called and invited me to a party at the Playboy mansion. Jake was scheduled to fly back to New York, but no way was he letting me go to the mansion without him.

Playboy sent a limousine to pick us up. I hadn't brought a lot of clothes to California, so I wore what I had; a white cotton jumpsuit with a zipper in front. The party was outdoors with sixty men and half as many women in attendance. There were a few bunny types, but most of the women worked for the company in a management capacity or came as dates.

Essentially, it was an office party, not a fantasy male bash. Except for the fact that Hugh Hefner was wandering around in silk pajamas with a pipe in one hand and a can of Pepsi in the other, it could have been IBM or Exxon instead of *Playboy*. The food was great. There were two bars. Everyone was friendly. Gary introduced me to Marilyn Grabowski, who was *Playboy*'s west coast photography editor, and I liked her. Hugh Hefner seemed excited to meet Jake and totally disinterested by me. Jake had to leave early to catch his flight and I left when he did. That was it, but I'd been impressed.

So when I got back to Miami and friends began asking, "What was it like? Are you going to do *Playboy?*" I wasn't sure what the answer would be.

Then Marilyn Grabowski started calling. She wasn't aggressive but she was persistent. "Vikki, there's an aura about you. You really should do it. Please, think about it. I'm sure it will be beautiful." And of course, there was the money, which was substantial, although no firm figure had been mentioned yet.

Weighing it all, I was confused and uncertain. As a child, I hadn't walked around naked in front of my own sisters. The first time I studied my body was after I'd gotten married. Even with Jake and Tony, I'd avoided casual nudity because being clothed most of the time made nudity seem more sensual and exciting. I needed help in making a decision, so I turned to the people who knew me best and would be affected most by what I did—my children.

Chris was the first one I talked with about it. "Do it," she said.

"Why?"

"Because this is more than just a photo layout. People think women lose their sexual desirability as they grow older, and you're living proof we don't. You're an inspiration to me. You inspire my girl-friends. Because of you, I'm not afraid of reaching fifty. Other women should benefit from that."

Next was Jack, and I was sure he'd feel differently. Jack is a stickler for protocol, very straight and rigid. "Mother," he said—that's the way he speaks to me—"Mother, you should do it."

"Why?"

"Because you have something to offer, and right now it's confined to a few people. If you do *Playboy*, you'll be making a statement and leading women to a better, happier way of life."

So now I had two children casting me as Moses leading women over fifty out of the wilderness into the promised land. Joey was vote number three. He's kind of a wild man, very emotional, the opposite of Jack. "Go for it," Joey told me. "Let it all hang out."

Harrison was the person I was most concerned about. The other kids were grown. He was eighteen years old. "Do it," he told me. "I won't be embarrassed. There's nothing wrong with posing for *Playboy*. You're a beautiful woman. I want you to do it."

I kept looking for negatives and not finding any that mattered. If the public didn't like it, so what? The people I loved, my family and friends, wanted me to do it. I had their support. I wouldn't be hurting anyone. And I needed the money. Meanwhile, Marilyn Grabowski kept calling. Finally, I told her yes.

Marilyn was ecstatic. "I'll get our best photographer," she promised. "When you come to Los Angeles, you'll stay at the mansion. The layout will be wonderful. I'm sure you'll love it."

Then came the waiting, and I began to get anxious. My mood kept changing. Sometimes in the middle of the night, I'd wake up and think, I can't do this. I'd call Chris, and she was like my mother. "Now stop being negative. I don't want to hear any more about it. You're going to California." Other times, I was excited. Oh my God, I can't wait. I'll wear something beautiful. The pictures will be wonderful.

Back and forth. Back and forth . . . Panic. I can't be serious. I'm not going to Los Angeles. I don't care how much money they pay me. I'll live in a tent before I take my clothes off for

Playboy . . . Excitement. Who made it a law that women over fifty aren't sexually desirable? Who force-feeds that propaganda to girls and makes them hold onto it as they get older? . . . Commitment. I said I'd do it. The decision is final. That's it, period.

I kept vacillating, wavering, going up and down like a see-saw, until finally it was time to fly to Los Angeles. On the plane, I was nervous; "paranoid" would be a better word for it. *Playboy* sent a limousine to meet me at the airport. The mansion had five guest bedrooms; each of them small, very plain and simple, but with a spectacular view of the mountains. My room had a double bed and dresser. A copy of the latest edition of *Playboy* was on the night table. Essentially, everything was set up like a resort hotel. Dinner was in the dining room at a set hour, but guests could eat in their rooms whenever they wanted. All we had to do was call the kitchen and choose from the day's menu. Each night, there was a different activity—backgammon, a movie, whatever. The help was personable.

My first full day, I got up, ate breakfast, and met Marilyn Grabowski at the mansion office. I was terribly nervous, telling myself over and over, I can't do this. Marilyn drove me to a studio, where a photographer named Ken Marcus was waiting. She kept saying, "Don't worry, you're going to be beautiful. We women need this. You have to do it for us, Vikki."

Ken introduced me to his assistants: a man and two women who handled wardrobe, make-up, and miscellaneous logistics. They put a little make-up on me; no more than I'd use going out at night. Meanwhile, I was telling myself to pretend I was someone else, not me. And I was dying, dying, dying. I wasn't worried about looking good. I was scared stiff about taking my clothes off.

Marilyn left and went back to the office. Ken sat me down on a chair for some test shots, and then started choosing my wardrobe. There was a huge closet full of bathing suits, negligees, and other revealing outfits. He and the others went through them, saying, "Yes, that's nice. No. No. Okay. This looks good." They put a headband made of shells around my forehead, supposedly because it had an earthy natural look. Then I tried on several costumes and the shooting started. At first, I was covered. But gradually, it was, "Pull the sleeve down a bit . . . Now take your arm out of the sleeve." Meanwhile, Ken's assistants were constantly pampering me, fixing my hair, making sure my makeup wasn't smeared. I like rhythm and blues music so, during the shooting, a tape of rhythm and blues was playing. They offered me wine but, during the first session, I didn't take any.

"Try to be comfortable . . . Vikki, the bathing suit looks lovely . . . Lower the strap . . . Lift your shoulder . . . "

Soon, the bikini top was half-off, which was okay because nothing was showing. Then it was, "Stretch your arm . . . Stand up; head to the left . . . lean forward . . ." until pretty soon something was showing, but it was hard to remember because my body was so twisted that I wasn't sure what I was doing.

Through it all, Ken Marcus stayed behind the camera. He wasn't socializing; just doing his job. The assistant kept running Polaroid shots over to Marilyn's office. Then she'd call to discuss them with Ken, directing the whole thing by telephone from behind her desk. Before the shooting, I'd told myself, either I do it or I don't. If I do, it's important to be free and natural. That was good in the abstract, but in reality it didn't work. I was terribly nervous. I kept trying to cover my breasts. When I was exposed, all I could think of was, let it be over. Hurry.

The first day's shooting lasted about four hours. Afterward, I was emotionally drained, exhausted. All I wanted was to go back to the mansion, soak in a hot tub, eat something for dinner, and go to sleep. Day number two was more of the same, except this time we shot in a different studio with a huge bed as the primary prop. I took one look, and decided there was only one way to get through it. I got loaded. Like the day before, they offered me wine. This time I took it. I get high on two glasses. On this particular occasion, I drank three. It did relax me. By any standard, I felt less inhibited than the day before. All morning, I kept telling myself, these pictures will be great because finally I'm comfortable. Then, late in the day, I saw the proofs. They were awful. I looked like a drunken lush.

So day three I was sober again. And the same conflicts I'd felt before were back to torment me. I'd be lying on the bed in some contorted position and find myself asking, what am I doing? I have four children. Look at me!

Whenever possible, when we weren't shooting, I wore a robe, a blanket, anything to cover me. Even while we shot, I'd hold a prop to give me the illusion of cover. Finally, at the very end, I took everything off. Ken was snapping photos. I was praying he'd go faster. And all I heard was, "Lift your right shoulder. Higher. A little lower. Now lift your head up more. Raise your eyebrows. Relax your mouth."

I didn't feel beautiful; not at all.

"Stretch your back. Arch your shoulders. Turn your head to the left. No, no, Vikki, that's wrong."

Then, mercifully, it ended. Three days of shooting; a thousand photos. Marilyn promised she'd send me the pictures that were chosen before they ran in the pictorial, and I flew back to Florida. A week later, a *Playboy* writer came to Miami to interview me for the text that would accompany the article. After that, I got a letter from Gary Cole, saying the pictures were "spectacular" and he'd send me copies as soon as the layout was complete.

All of that took place in May. Then . . . nothing. No telephone calls. No pictures. May turned to June, and I began to feel apprehensive. July came and went, and still I didn't know what the photos looked like. Finally, in mid-August, *Playboy* mailed me a Xerox layout. There were no captions, no headings or text. Just grainy black-and-white copies of sixteen photos. And to put it mildly, I was upset. Eight of the photos were reproductions of black and white pictures from my family album. Jake and me; me and the kids. Those were fine. Seven more were color shots from the Los Angeles sessions. I'd assumed *Playboy* would choose the most beautiful photos. Now it was clear they'd opted for the most revealing. But I'd understood the nature of the magazine when I agreed to pose; so regarding those seven, I had no complaint.

The last photo was mortifying. As I said earlier, Ken Marcus had a large wardrobe at his studio. For most of the shooting, he'd told me what to wear (or not wear). However, toward the end of the last session, he'd let me pick my own costume. The choice was easy. Years before, when I worked at the Latin Quarter, I'd had three uniforms—an elegant gown, a regular chorus girl outfit, and a mesh net costume with feathers. Ken's wardrobe had an almost identical fishnet, albeit without feathers. That's what I'd chosen. It didn't cover much. The nylon stretched, so it was almost as revealing as wearing nothing. But the mesh extended from my wrists to my ankles, which gave me the illusion of being covered.

Now, I was sitting in my living room, looking at a picture of me in the nylon mesh. And I panicked. Because in addition to feathers, the costume at the Latin Quarter had a piece of cloth covering the crotch. I'd thought Ken's suit had a similar piece, and apparently it hadn't.

The result? A photograph that pictured me with my legs spread apart and nothing covering my crotch.

I was frantic. I didn't know what to do. I stared at the photo, not fully believing, telling myself, Vikki, this time you've really done it. Finally, I picked up the telephone and called Jack. He had a good business head. I trusted his judgment. Jack came over. My own son; I was embarrassed. How could I show him the photo? But he was very matter-of-fact, like a priest or a doctor.

"Let me see it, mother. I have to see it to know what you're talking about."

I gave him the photo and went into another room while he looked at it. Then I came back.

"It's very revealing," Jack told me. "Maybe they shouldn't use it."

"I know, but how can I stop it?"

"Why did you let them take a picture like that?"

"I thought there was a piece of cloth, like my costume at the Latin Quarter. There must have been or else I wouldn't have spread my legs. Probably, they retouched it."

That was it! *Playboy* had retouched the photo. So together, Jack and I telephoned Gary Cole and told him the other photos were all right but I didn't like the way they'd altered the one of me in the fishnet. "There was a piece of cloth over the crotch, Gary. You retouched it."

Gary was adamant. "No, Vikki, we did not retouch it. That's what you were wearing. It's impossible to airbrush under mesh. And it's much too late to change the layout."

Next, I telephoned Marilyn Grabowski.

"Vikki, honestly, we didn't airbrush the photo. The only retouching was on another picture where a vein was showing on the side of your neck. Don't you remember? We wanted an honest natural look. *Playboy* wouldn't be selling you if you had to be made over."

Two days later, a long letter arrived from Gary. "Dear Vikki, It would truly be an understatement to say that everyone here at *Playboy* is concerned about your feelings toward the feature. I in particular am distressed that I may have played a part in causing you some unhappiness. I will do whatever I can to try to make you feel better. Unfortunately, changing the pictures is not one of the possibilities." The letter went on, offering no relief, voicing the view that, "Everything need not be so bleak. Despite your reaction of the moment, the consensus is the feature is gorgeous. Probably, no one will look at it as critically or with the same sensitivity to some aspects of it as you and your sons."

So that was *Playboy*'s answer. And frankly, I was starting to question whether they had dealt with me in good faith. The pictorial was scheduled for the November issue, which went on sale in late September. It was now the first week of September. And still, no one had shown me color photos. Marilyn Grabowski called several more times seeking to lay my fears to rest. "Trust me, Vikki. The picture in color isn't the way you think it is. There's nothing wrong. Everything is in good taste."

Maybe; maybe not. But I did have one trump card left. For whatever reason, *Playboy* had failed to finalize my contract. I don't know whether it was sloppy bookkeeping or the fact that they wanted to see how the photos turned out before they paid me or what. But the bottom line was, I'd never signed a release. That meant, at the same time Gary Cole was telling me it was too late to remove the fishnet picture, I might have been able to kill the whole feature.

There were quite a few family discussions that week. But in the end, I decided to do what I thought was honorable. I signed the release, trusting their claim that the photo hadn't been retouched. Then, with more than a little anxiety, I sat back and waited for the storm.

The magazine went on sale in late September. To eliminate the possibility that anyone might miss the feature, the cover had my name in large pink letters above the tag-line "Raging Bull's Woman Is 51 And A Knockout." The text accompanying the pictorial was more than complimentary. "Vikki LaMotta has one of the ten great bodies in the world," it read. "Her face is perfect. She's a composite of all the women John Derek has married. And she's fifty-one years old."

That was the hook—fifty-one years old. For most of my life, I hadn't thought about age. Now, suddenly, everyone was asking, "How do you look the way you look? What kind of make-up do you use? What do you eat? How do you exercise? Do you realize you were twenty-seven years old when this month's centerfold was born?"

I was still unhappy with the fishnet photo, but it wasn't as bad in color as I'd thought. Jake was more upset than I was. Right after the magazine went on sale, he telephoned to report, "I just saw *Playboy*, and I don't think I can stand it."

"Jake, you were the one who told me to do it. Did you think I was posing for *Ladies' Home Journal*?"

"I know what I said, but seeing it upsets me. I don't like

other men being able to look at you like that."

Everyone else in the family reacted positively. Joey told me that his friends kept asking, "Is that really your Mom? Can you get me a date?" Someone else might have been embarrassed but he liked it. Jack and Harrison both said they were pleased. Chris's ex-husband sent me a congratulatory note. Then I heard from Jake's mother; eighty-four years old, a woman who always walks around carrying a Bible. "Vikki," she told me, "times have changed; people are different now. Good for you." Mama LaMotta also volunteered some financial advice. "You look so beautiful. You should do a brassiere commercial like that lady with the big bosom, Jane Russell. You'd be very good in that commercial."

Basically, I'd expected the reaction I got from my family. But I wasn't prepared for the media response. The fact that I was fifty-one made the pictorial a phenomenon. *Newsweek* ran two items with photos in its "Newsmakers" section. Newspapers across the country followed suit. *Playboy* reported more newsstand sales of the issue to women than any other in the history of the magazine. Cashing in on the obvious, they hired me for a ten-day promotional tour, starting with a Tom Brokaw interview on *The Today Show* in New York. In city after city, the reception was wonderful. I'd assumed there would be substantial negative reaction, that people would be critical. But everyone I came in contact with was supportive.

One woman came up to me and asked, "Can I thank you?"

I said, "Yeah, you can thank me. Why?"

"For letting all those men out there know women our age are still sexual. This'll show them."

Another woman told me, "Vikki, when I got married, I

wasn't sure I wanted children because of what it would do to my body. But having seen how you look, I'm not afraid anymore."

In Los Angeles, San Francisco, Chicago, everywhere I went, people (and particularly women) couldn't have been nicer. "I have your picture pasted on the refrigerator as an inspiration to diet" . . . "Our exercise instructor put a photo of you on the bulletin board as a goal to work toward" . . . "Please, could I have an autographed photo of you for my boyfriend. He says he's in love with you."

I got letters from doctors and lawyers asking for dates and a prom invitation from a high school senior in Niagara Falls. One woman wrote, inquiring where she could buy a fishnet suit like the one I'd worn. She wanted to put it on for her husband, who kept raving about that particular photo. Quite a few people wrote expounding their religious views. Amazingly, none of them were critical. But the recurring theme, over and over, came from women who wrote that I'd released them from the fear of aging.

After the tour, I was offered several movie roles. The most promising came from Home Box Office. But when I read the script, there was too much nudity. Obviously, they wanted to capitalize on *Playboy*. The money was good but I told myself, enough is enough. Then I got a call from an editor at *High Society*, who offered $25,000 for a set of photos. I'd never heard of the magazine, so I asked what they had in mind and he told me, "Well, there is some nudity but it's quite elegant and tastefully done." That conjured up images of the social register and evening gowns with a provocative look but nothing unseemly. I told him maybe, that I'd have to see the magazine first.

That afternoon, I went out to buy a copy of *High Society*.

There was a bookstore near where I lived that had a large collection of magazines up front and a small X-rated section in back. I knew the owner. He was a quiet man in his late thirties with thinning hair, very serious and polite, the sort of person who never smiles. When *Raging Bull* was released, he'd saved all the magazine articles for me. I walked into the store and asked very openly, "Do you have a magazine called *High Society*?" He said yes, in back.

"You mean, with those other magazines?"

"That's right. Are you in *High Society* too this month?"

"No, but I'm thinking about it."

Anyway, I went to the back of the store, and still I didn't realize what I was looking for. He must have put it on the wrong rack, I told myself. Then I saw the magazine, picked it up, and started leafing through the pages. It was trash. I just put it down and walked out.

The editor called for my answer two days later, and I told him no thank you. Then he raised the offer to $50,000.

"Look, *High Society* is not the type of magazine I want to be in."

"We'll go higher. Name your price."

"There is no price."

There were offers from other men's magazines later, but I turned them all down. Even though I'd posed for *Playboy*, I wasn't interested in making the rounds. Then, gradually, the furor subsided and I returned to being a private citizen instead of a prospective centerfold.

On balance, I'm pleased with the way *Playboy* worked out. But I'd be less than honest if I didn't admit to mixed feelings. Some of the things the magazine stands for do bother me. Too many men deal with women only as sex objects. And despite Hugh Hefner's "liberated" philosophy, that's a lot of what the magazine is about. The pictorials tend to place women, myself included, in a subservient position; one that a certain kind of man finds uncomplicated and attractive. To the extent my participation reinforced that view of women, I can only say, that wasn't my intent.

Also, posing for *Playboy* did complicate my life. Ever since adolescence, I've had to put up with men mentally undressing me. Now it's worse. I'm constantly in situations where I meet people who've seen photos of me naked. At times it's embarrassing, and too often it leads to preconceptions about me that aren't accurate. If the subject comes up, I try to explain that posing for *Playboy* was one act, not part of my everyday life. But not everyone sees it that way, and I have to be careful, particularly on dates, about the signals I send out. That's unfortunate, but it's my own doing. *Playboy* was my choice.

Still, there are things I'm satisfied with regarding my experience with *Playboy*. All my life, I'd met people who thought that sensuality was dependent on age; that women begin to deteriorate when they reach thirty; that the most desirable women have youth on their side. And women believe it. They walk differently when they turn thirty. They cut their hair short because they're told long hair looks silly on older women. They begin to act old because they think they're old; and as a result, they become old. I hope my posing for *Playboy* changed that for some women. I wanted to show that older women don't have to concede anything in the area of sexual desirability; that women of fifty can be just as attractive, and sometimes more so, than they were at twenty; that what comes after forty is just as important as what comes before it; that women don't lose their allure at twenty-nine or thirty-nine or forty-nine or ever.

I know there are people who don't approve of what I did. It's not hard to imagine what they're saying. "Vikki LaMotta wasn't showing people her convictions when she posed for *Playboy*. She was showing them her breasts ... There are plenty of women struggling to get by who don't make money by posing nude ... What an ego. This lady must think she's really great."

Well, I don't think I'm great because I posed for *Playboy*. I don't need that ego trip, and never did. I wouldn't have done it if my children were young, and I wouldn't have done it if I hadn't needed the money. Also, I understand that what's right for me isn't necessarily right for someone else. Everybody has their own philosophy of life. I'll honor yours, and I hope you honor mine.

For example, I'm much less active sexually than a lot of single women. If I have a steady boyfriend, someone I'm involved with, that's one thing. But I'm not promiscuous. I won't sleep with someone just because it's been a while. There was a time when I had a few purely sexual flings, but those days are long gone. Some people who meet me see the way I look, they know I posed for *Playboy*, and right away they make assumptions. Then they start to trade in rumors. "Oh yeah, Vikki LaMotta; she put the make on me" or "I hear Vikki balled so-and-so." It's garbage but there are fools who believe it because it feeds their fantasies. Simply put, I have no intention of ruining my sex life by sleeping around.

Also, I don't go out with married men. That's partly for moral reasons and partly because, if I'm with someone, I don't want to share him. It's not a turn-on for me to be with a man who's thinking about another woman. If she means more to him than I do, if he feels guilty about being with me, I don't want him. Some women have no objection to dating married men. So, hey, you make your choice and I'll make mine. And having decided how I'll live my life, the truth is I've had zero problems with men's wives. If I meet a man and woman who are together, whether they're married or not, I try to relate to the woman first. I want her to know that she's as important to me as the man. Then, if she seems jealous or doesn't want me around, I disappear very quickly; goodbye.

I'm aware that nudity has its boundaries. For example, the *Playboy* photos are included in my scrapbook but they're closely cropped. I'm not embarrassed by them in a proper setting, but there are improper settings too. For instance, suppose a reporter comes over for an interview, looks at my scrapbook, and sees me with my breasts hanging out. I'd rather not have that. Or if a friend's children are turning the pages, looking at articles about *Raging Bull*, and there I am with my bare breasts. That wouldn't be right.

But the people who judge me harshly for doing *Playboy* weren't paying my bills. Back in 1981, I was simply trying to be self-supporting without asking my friends, my family, or the government for financial help. My looks were an asset and I used them to make money. Obviously, there are limits to the degree I'm willing to trade on my looks. I've never slept with anyone for favors—and believe me, it's been offered. I wouldn't lead a man on with hints of sex if I didn't mean it. Agreed, many women wouldn't pose nude regardless of circumstances. But then they'll have to find some other way to support themselves, and I might not approve of their choice.

In the end then, I'm glad I did *Playboy*. It was a positive experience. There was something to be said about women and aging, and the pictorial said it. Although at the same time, I have to say that, for me at least, *Playboy* was one of the less sexual things I've done.

Playboy used me; I know that. But I wasn't an impressionable nineteen-year-old who posed without considering the consequences, and I got fair value in return. The truth is, writing this book makes me feel far more exposed than being photographed naked. And the truth also is that sometimes, even now, I'll wake up in the middle of the night and tell myself, I can't believe I did *Playboy*.

Vikki and her son Harrison Foster.

Coming Home

Chapter Fifteen

After *Playboy*, certain things changed. All my life, I'd been used to attention but often it came from being an appendage to someone else. I'd been Jake's wife, Sam's girlfriend, an accessory to *Raging Bull*. Now I was a mini-celebrity in my own right. People who'd ignored me began to stop on the street to say hello. People who had said hello suddenly wanted to have dinner. People I'd had dinner with wanted to be my best friend. Still, the basics remained unchanged. My friends and family treated me the same. To them, nothing was different. That's the way it should be. When I go home at night, when I'm with people I care about, it has nothing to do with the fact that someone I've never met might know my name.

During the year after *Playboy*, I made quite a few personal appearances at conventions and on television. Then I was approached by an advertising agency that wanted me to serve as spokeswoman for a line of cosmetics and skin-care products. I agreed and, in 1983, Vikki LaMotta Cosmetics was formed. It's a small company, selling primarily through cable television commercials and via direct mail. For a while, I helped operate the business from my home in Miami but that meant commuting regularly to New York. Finally, in late 1983, I moved to Manhattan. I love it. I'm home.

My life is more settled now than ever before. I'm not wealthy. My income from the company is modest but enough to get by. I don't go out much. Spending time on the telephone with someone I care about in Florida makes more sense to me than having two drinks in a bar. I enjoy dinner at nice restaurants and occasional dancing with friends. Basically though, I stay close to home. I don't have a lot of material possessions. My wardrobe is what it's been for years. One thing I do miss about Miami is being able to go bike-riding or down to the beach on a whim. There's no open space near my home in Manhattan. That makes exercising a hassle. I don't like aerobics; I'm not into jogging. Three or four times a week, I do stretching exercises and work with weights at a gym. I walk a lot and swim.

Now that I'm alone, I lead a more selfish life than before. One of the first things I noticed after moving to New York was, when I went to the supermarket, everything in the shopping-cart was for me. I didn't like it. I still don't. Over the years, I grew so used to doing things for other people that it seems unnatural to do things only for myself. When the kids were young, I looked forward to their being grown and out on their own. Like every other mother, I got tired of coming home and finding the house a mess. Now I come home, everything is exactly the way I left it, and it feels wrong.

Family is the most important thing in the world to me. My brother Harvey is retired from the New York City Police Department. Don runs an air-conditioning repair shop in Houston. Pat and her husband own a construction company in Queens. Phyllis moved to Florida after her husband retired from his job with a limousine service in Westchester. My brother Joe lives in Manhattan and works for a firm that supplies management personnel to hotels.

As for the children, they're grown now. Jack has been quite successful financially. He's an executive with a company that owns a nationwide chain of liquor stores, discos, and bars. All his life, he sacrificed to become financially secure, and it shows. He owns a beautiful house outside of Philadelphia and his investments are sound. Joey has worked as a maitre d' and restaurant manager in Miami. Chris is the hostess at a restaurant in New York. Harrison is in Atlanta, where he's a graduate of Georgia State University and working two jobs while he looks for one good one.

My mother lives in Queens with my sister Pat. Long after my father died, she went out briefly with a family friend. Since then, I don't think she's dated and I can't picture her with anyone besides Feebie. Recently, I was going through a box of mementos and came across some postcards she'd sent me with notes like, "The view of the mountains is beautiful from here; Love, Mother" . . . "We just went for a ride on this boat; Love, Mother" . . . The cards were postmarked 1979, when I was forty-nine years old. I'd kept them. I guess, even now, I want to imagine myself with her, looking at the mountains, boating on a lake; things we seldom shared when I was a child.

My father has been gone for a quarter-century, and I still miss him. I know he loved me and also that there were many sides to him. Often, I wish I could bring him back, even if it were just for a day. He loved to eat; he loved being pampered. If I could see him again, I'd cook a big meal, we'd talk, and I'd ask the questions I never asked him. How did he and my mother meet? What did he enjoy in life? And what about the bad things he did? Could I have acted differently to help him?

As for lovers, first and foremost there's Jake. Sam was murdered; shot seven times in 1975. Over the years, I've been largely out of touch with Tony. Other men have come and gone, but Jake has run through forty years of my life; his obsession and, I guess, mine.

I still care about Jake and always will, although not the way he wants me to. He's family. We had three children together. Once, there was passion between us but the fire is gone. Now, when I see Jake, I feel sad. He needed help. All he knew was violence and anger. But what makes me saddest is that he didn't enjoy life. I don't think he had fun living. Jake could go anywhere on this planet, see the most beautiful sights in the world, and his observation would be, "So what? You mean we have to go all the way up that hill to see The Parthenon? We have to climb those stairs to see the Sistine Chapel?"

Jake has been married six times. First there was Ida. Then Vikki, Sally, Dimitri, Debbie, and Theresa, in that order. That's a lot of wives. Yet to this day, he maintains an insatiable curiosity and possessiveness about me. Two years ago, I was invited to an Italian-American Sports Hall of Fame dinner. Jake was there too. After dinner, I was talking with Dan Marino, the quarterback for the Miami Dolphins. I'd lived in Miami for twenty-eight years. The most natural thing in the world was for us to chat. And right away, I could see Jake fuming. He was livid; smoke was practically coming out of his nostrils. After the party, he told me, "Vikki, you're disgusting. How could you stand there and talk to Dan Marino?"

"Jake, I'm not your date. We're not married. I'm free. I'm single. I can talk to anyone I want."

"I don't care. This guy, Marino, he's twenty-five years old. I only want you talking to guys older than you are."

I couldn't believe it. All I could say was, "Gee, Jake, that's pretty old. There aren't many people as old as me. Maybe you could give me a break and let me talk with someone who's forty-nine or fifty."

Still, Jake's influence is very much a part of me. He had a major impact on my life, and I still use his name. After we were divorced, I went back to my maiden name, Thailer. When Tony and I got married, I became Vikki Foster. But after Tony, I reverted to Vikki LaMotta. Three of my children were named "LaMotta". The house, the car, my bank account, and who knows what else belonged to "Vikki LaMotta." Plus, I like the name. It's mine as much as Jake's.

Even now, despite everything, there are times when I feel fondly toward Jake. Some part of me will always wish that he could have been different; that we could have built on the excitement between us to forge a life for ourselves and our children. That didn't happen though, and what I'm left with are some hard lessons.

I'm just starting to realize now how much scar tissue I have; how my parents, Jake, and a few other people shaped me. When I look back from decade to decade, it's hard to believe it all happened to one person. The little girl who hung out at the cab stand with Willy Goldberg, who married Jake and dated Sam; the fifteen-year-old who was raped, worked at The 181 Club, and had her hair cut off by her father; the woman who posed for *Playboy* and was present at the creation of *Raging Bull*; the chorus girl, the mother. They're all me, and I have no idea what will happen tomorrow.

There are times when I wish I was more sure of what to do. Sometimes I think I should just let myself be led wherever I'm going to be led. But then I'll say to myself, wait a minute, that's wrong. I'll face situations that seem the same as ones I faced years ago. But they're not, because I'm different now and the people I'm dealing with are different too. I realize that I've made mistakes in life, mostly from feeling when I should have thought and thinking when I should have followed my feelings. But like anyone else, I can change my life if I want to. We are what we fight to become.

One thing I've become adamant about though, is staying away from negative people. Bad times are part of life, but some people dwell on the negative. They hold onto their misery; and after a while, it rubs off on everyone they deal with. Being around negative people never made me happy. I learned that the hard way.

If there's a gap in my life today, it's the absence of a truly satisfying relationship with a man. What I'm talking about is something rare; not just a marriage that lasts for twenty or thirty years because it's there; not a relationship where the spouses are "faithful" because it's the proper thing to do. I'm talking about love.

I don't think I've ever loved anyone in a mature adult way. Maybe that's because, when I was a child, there was no role model to follow. I'm sure there are other reasons too. Regardless, I know there's a chance that I won't meet someone to be with "till death do us part." Both of my marriages were so bad that sometimes I question whether I have the strength and courage to try again. But in my heart, I feel I'm warm enough, soft enough, smart enough, and good enough; that I have everything to offer. To be with one person as lover and friend, to share everything with honesty and trust; that to me is the ultimate gift. Not that I need a man in my life to be happy. I don't. But the type of relationship I'm talking about would be a joy.

There's time. Aging was never meant to dictate cutting back on the pleasures of life; only a full embrace of living. I'm not a fifty-seven-year-old woman with dreams of being thirty again. I'm a fifty-seven-year-old woman trying to act fifty-seven. The greatest tragedy of my life would be to go from infancy to old age without reaching maturity. If I'd been born with the knowledge to do everything right, I wouldn't have made the mistakes I made. But look at a baby; any baby. We all start out knowing nothing and we learn.

The way I look at it then is, there have been good times and bad, happy and sad. I'm not a star. All I want is to be somebody's lover, somebody's neighbor, my children's mother, somebody's friend. On occasion, a man or woman I've never met will come up to me on the street and ask for an autograph or simply say hello. When that happens, I ask myself, if I were this person how would I want to be treated. I'll talk with them, whether it's for thirty seconds, a minute, two minutes, whatever. I'll ask their name and what they do for a living; look them in the eye. I want to give myself every opportunity to like them and for them to like me. And when we're done, if they smile and say, "I can't wait to tell my husband I met you," or, "Wait till I tell the guys at the bowling alley," I feel that both of us have lived a shade better.

Life is wonderful. I want to live it.

Vikki LaMotta
New York City
1987

Afterword: 2006

As Vikki LaMotta was growing older, the significant people in her life weren't standing still in that matter.

Jake LaMotta has lived a long life and resides in New York City, where he enjoys his status as a ring icon. *Raging Bull* has given him fame and acceptance forever.

Tony Foster died of a heart attack in 1990 at age 59. At the time, he was working as an entertainment director for a Miami hotel and still sang occasionally in clubs. "He never stopped caring about my mother," their son Harrison says. "And to his credit, he never said anything negative to me about her."

Vikki's mother died in 1999. "The *Playboy* thing was a shock for her," Harrison recalls. "It distanced them even further from each other and they never really reconciled."

Two of Vikki's children were felled by tragedy. Jack LaMotta enjoyed continued business success and, in his late-thirties, moved to his dream house in eastern Pennsylvania. Then he was diagnosed with stomach cancer and died in 1998 at age 51. Joey LaMotta worked at a series of jobs and eventually joined with Jake to promote a mail-order business that sold LaMotta's Tomato Sauce. He was one of 229 people killed in the crash of Swiss Air 111 off the coast of Nova Scotia in 1998. Several years before his death, Joey and Vikki were able to reunite with his daughter, Kim-Marie.

Vikki's daughter, Chris, still lives in Manhattan. She never remarried but has been in a long-term relationship for several decades.

Harrison Foster became a portrait photographer and, in 1997, founded Harrison Photography with his fiancée Heather Armstrong. They moved to Florida and got married. On July 20, 2004, their daughter Lilyana was born.

"For most of my life, my girlfriends were freaked out by my mother," Harrison acknowledges. "They were intimidated by her way of doing things and how beautiful she was. In Heather, I found a woman who was strong enough to deal with it, and my two best friends became friends."

As for Vikki, she left New York in 1992 and moved back to Florida, where she lived in a condominium with a spectacular view of the ocean in Boca Raton. Financially, she derived income from Vikki LaMotta Cosmetics and occasional memorabilia shows and was well-provided for by Jack's estate.

"My mother didn't go out a lot," Harrison says. "She hung out at home. She was a prolific reader. There were no new romantic involvements in her life. But she was in a healthy beautiful environment and she was content."

Several days after Lilyana Foster was born, Vikki collapsed while out shopping. She had suffered a tear in her aortic valve and underwent eight hours of emergency surgery at Holy Cross Hospital. Three months of intensive in-patient physical therapy followed. Vikki's motivation for living, she said, was the desire to bond with her newborn granddaughter.

"Finally, my mother's condition improved to the point where she was able to go home," Harrison remembers. "It was remarkable that she was still alive. But it was hard for her. She had always been a very independent woman, and she was no longer able to do things the way she'd once been able to. But she was still a joy in my life. And thank God, she and Lilyana had time to bond."

On January 24, 2005, Vikki suffered another aortic dissection. Harrison was in Alabama for a photography shoot and began the twelve-hour drive to Boca Raton. While he was on the road, Heather called and told him that his mother had died.

"I'll always miss her," Harrison says. "And I'll always be strengthened by the gifts she gave me. My mother was full of life and she taught me to enjoy life. I love the fact that I never saw her talk down to or disrespect anyone. And even in her seventies, she was still a knockout."